Perfect Memory Training

Dr Fiona McPherson has a PhD in psychology, and has spent many years researching how to improve human memory. She lives in Wellington, New Zealand, where she runs a small research company with her partner, and publishes an e-zine about memory.

Other titles in the *Perfect* series

Perfect Answers to Interview Questions – Max Eggert
Perfect Babies' Names – Rosalind Fergusson
Perfect Brain Training – Philip Carter
Perfect Best Man – George Davidson
Perfect Calorie Counting – Kate Santon
Perfect Confidence – Jan Ferguson
Perfect CV – Max Eggert
Perfect Detox – Gill Paul
Perfect Family Quiz – David Pickering
Perfect Letters and Emails for All Occasions – George Davidson
Perfect Numerical Test Results – Joanna Moutafi and Ian Newcombe
Perfect Numerical and Logical Test Results – Joanna Moutafi and Marianna Moutafi
Perfect Party Games – Stephen Curtis
Perfect Personality Profiles – Helen Baron
Perfect Persuasion – Richard Storey
Perfect Positive Thinking – Lynn Williams
Perfect Presentations – Andrew Leigh and Michael Maynard
Perfect Psychometric Test Results – Joanna Moutafi and Ian Newcombe
Perfect Pub Quiz – David Pickering
Perfect Punctuation – Stephen Curtis
Perfect Readings for Weddings – Jonathan Law
Perfect Relaxation – Elaine van der Zeil
Perfect Speeches for All Occasions – Matt Shinn
Perfect Wedding Planning – Cherry Chappell
Perfect Wedding Speeches and Toasts – George Davidson
Perfect Weight Loss – Kate Santon
Perfect Written English – Chris West

Perfect
Memory Training

Fiona McPherson

Published by Random House Books 2009
2 4 6 8 10 9 7 5 3 1

First published in Great Britain in 2009 by
Random House Books
Random House, 20 Vauxhall Bridge Road,
London SW1V 2SA

www.rbooks.co.uk

Addresses for companies within The Random House Group Limited can be found at: www.randomhouse.co.uk/offices.htm

The Random House Group Limited Reg. No. 954009

A CIP catalogue record for this book
is available from the British Library

ISBN 9781847945365

The Random House Group Limited supports The Forest Stewardship Council (FSC), the leading international forest certification organisation. All our titles that are printed on Greenpeace approved FSC certified paper carry the FSC logo. Our paper procurement policy can be found at www.rbooks.co.uk/environment

Typeset in Minion by Palimpsest Book Production Limited,
Grangemouth, Stirlingshire
Printed and bound in Great Britain by CPI Bookmarque, Croydon, Surrey CR0 4TD

Contents

Part two: Strategies

Quick Reference Section

Introduction

I started thinking about memory from a practical rather than academic standpoint when lack of sleep and complete distraction started attacking my ability to think and remember. Having just completed a doctorate in cognitive psychology (the branch of psychology devoted to memory and how we think), it was with considerable surprise that I realised I knew nothing that helped me improve a failing memory. So I began to look at some less academic books that claimed to help improve memory.

What really struck me was that most books spouted the same few bits of advice which went back decades to the early days of experimental psychology, and even further back to the days of ancient Greece. Good advice in its time, but cognitive psychology has come a long way since then. So I looked, and I found that, indeed, there was some very useful, practical advice that hadn't made it out into the world. One finding in particular really stayed with me: that most memory improvement programmes don't have any permanent effect.

Why not? Why do people who try to improve their memory fail to do so? Not because they are unintelligent or lazy, but because the memory improvement programmes are flawed. They are based on effective strategies and valid principles, but they don't work because they have put in the 'too-hard' basket the information that you need to know to improve your memory.

You need to understand the context of what you're learning so that you know how and why the memory-improvement strategies work. Research suggests that whether you habitually and appropriately use effective memory strategies – and that's what permanent memory improvement is all about – depends far more on how much you know about your own memory processes than on how smart you are.

The first half of this book aims to fill this gap, by explaining the principles of memory, and the second half puts this knowledge into practice by explaining some strategies to improve your memory.

One of the reasons behind the failure of most memory improvement programmes to achieve long-lasting improvement is that 'memory' is really a category, like 'sport'. Would you say, 'I want to improve my sport'? Of course not. But you might say, 'I want to improve my tennis (or golf or swimming . . .)'.

Memory is not one thing. The feats of memory that so impress us are not evidence of a 'photographic' memory or any other innate talent. Being able to memorise a string of 80 digits after seeing them once is a trick anyone can learn – if they wish to devote months of training and practising to the skill.

But the trick does not generalise to other types of memory. The person who sweats for months to master longer and longer strings of digits will be no better at remembering shopping lists. Chess experts take years to develop their phenomenal memory for the arrangement of chess pieces, but that doesn't make them any better at remembering a speech or what they did last Tuesday.

Surveys have found that there are over 100 memory tasks in everyday life that can cause people problems. Each of these tasks requires a different strategy.

Don't panic! One hundred sounds a lot but think for a moment how many different techniques you have for simply getting through the day. Putting on your shoes is a different technique than putting on a shirt; making breakfast is an entirely different skill to cleaning your teeth. You probably use 100 different skills before you've gone out the door!

Moreover, you're not starting from scratch. You already know many memory skills, and you're probably quite happy with your level of competence at some of them. What it comes down to is identifying your needs. Don't say, 'I want to improve my memory'; say, 'I want to improve these specific memory skills'.

Part one of *Perfect Memory Training* will give you a good general understanding of how memory works, so that the different learning strategies in part two make much more sense. You will remember them more easily and be able to adapt them to different situations, because you understand why they work and which aspects are important. Once you understand why the strategies work, you will have greater confidence in using them.

Although I have emphasised that you cannot improve 'memory' but must target specific memory skills, that doesn't mean that memory skills should be acquired in a vacuum. You can learn to cook without any understanding of basic chemistry, but you'll be far better at adapting recipes and creating new ones if you understand the roles of the various ingredients (for example, whether the eggs are included to thicken, to bind, or to leaven).

Research has found that people are most likely to successfully apply appropriate learning and remembering strategies when they have also been taught general information about how the mind works. The more you understand about how memory works, the more likely you are to benefit from instruction in particular memory skills.

Part one

How memory works

1 Making memories

To understand how memory works, you need to understand what memory *is*. Clues to the hidden workings of the mind can be seen in the mistakes we make.

The other day I had to take the cat to the vet. While out I planned to return a library book and post some letters. I put the letters and the book on the seat next to me. The cat went in the back and wailed piteously. In a hurry to get home, distracted by the cat, I stopped beside the postbox and grabbed the letters to post. Just about to release them into the hole, I froze. I was about to post my library book. (Well, it was quite a thin one.)

Now certainly part of the reason for this mistake was that I was in a hurry and distracted. If your mind's not on the job, if you're operating on 'automatic pilot', this sort of mistake is common. But saying I wasn't paying attention doesn't really explain why this sort of mistake happens.

These mistakes happen because your actions are based on what's in your head, not directly on the world. In my head, there wasn't a library book, nor a pile of letters. Instead my mind had created two INTERNAL REPRESENTATIONS, with properties of their own – not necessarily, and certainly not entirely, the properties that the things themselves had. I knew, when I was creating the representation, that it didn't need to be remembered for very long. I also knew that there were only two attributes that were of interest: where it was; and what I was going to do with it.

And there you have the nub of the problem. Two representations in my mind: one reads 'sitting on front passenger seat' and 'post it'; the other reads 'sitting on front passenger seat' and 'return it to library'. Given that I wasn't paying any attention to the particular things that were sitting on the front passenger seat, I had a 50 per cent chance of getting it right.

Remembering is not simply about finding automatically stored replicas of things that you have experienced. Memories are CODES, and the type of code, or internal representation, that a memory has does not depend on the memory itself, but on how you coded it. Any memory can be coded in a number of different ways. The particular code you create for it will determine how easily you will find it later.

It also determines *what* you find. In the outside world the object might be a library book called *The Psychology of Anomalous Experience* by Graham Reed, in an orange and grey paperback, about a centimetre thick, about 12 by 20 centimetres in size, about 25 years old. But my memory code is based on what I consider important and relevant, to me, in the particular circumstances. In this case, my memory code may not have included any permanent attributes of the object, merely two entirely temporary ones: present location and my intention with it. What you find in memory, what you remember, is a matter of the memory code you created in the first place.

How memories are created

It's a common myth that everything you have ever experienced is recorded in loving and exact detail in the neurons of your brain. If it were true, where would the line be drawn?

Look around the room. Have you recorded for posterity every mark on the floor, every dustball? Look away, then back again. Have you made another recording?

Imagine everything experienced, no understanding needed, no picking and choosing of what's important, *everything* being stored holus-bolus. Every time a baby wakes, the scene, the sights, the sounds, the smells, the feeling of cloth against skin, the feeling of moving muscles, of bowel motions . . . all of it faithfully recorded. Every detail repeated again and again as it is experienced anew: Every minute? Every second? Every millisecond?

Without selection, without the focus of attention picking and choosing what's worth keeping and what's not, there is an infinity of information to be stored. Indeed, who says the baby has to wake? Even asleep, sounds, smells, feelings in the skin and muscles, can be perceived.

The first, most fundamental point about memory is that memory codes are created from selected information. We are not blank slates waiting to be written on, receiving every detail with humble gratitude. We are *users* of information, and the first thing we do with information is choose what to keep. You can choose whether your memory is a junk heap or a storage system.

If we remembered every single thing then quite possibly memory would be a junk heap – an attic into which everything is thrown higgledy-piggledy, 'for a rainy day'. And, like that attic, searching such a memory would be a time-consuming, frustrating business. Unless of course we had recently stored it away and it was by the door.

But memory is a structure. It has been constructed; is being reconstructed. Laws constrain and guide the building process. If your memory seems like an attic full of junk, it's because you don't understand the design principles.

The code principle

We associate things together in our minds. You say *bread* and I say *butter*; you say *cat* and I say *dog*. So familiar is this characteristic of our mental processes, we tend to take it for granted. But this ability is telling us something important about how we think and remember. The associations we make reflect the way our memory codes are organised. This is the code principle: that memories are selected and manipulated to *represent* experiences, not *reproduce* them.

The network principle

On paper we may draw a number of dots, so:

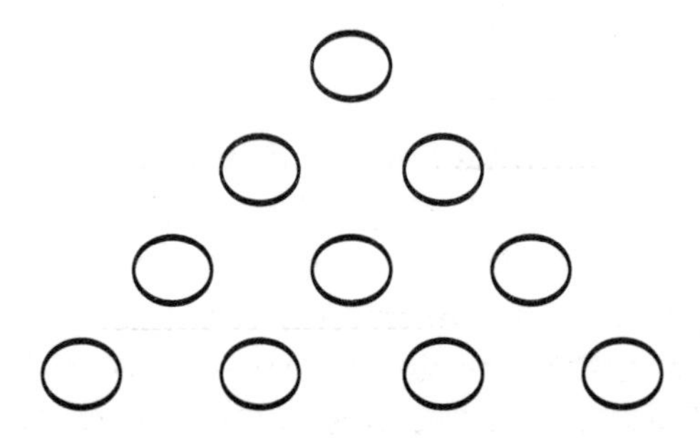

and we see a pyramid. But in the world outside the mind, the pyramid doesn't exist. It exists on paper only because we mentally 'fill in' the lines connecting the dots. Without these lines, the dots are not a pyramid, are not any sort of structure. They are simply a scattering of dots.

'Memory' is the name we give to our collection of memory codes. But, unlike our pyramid of dots, memory *is* a structure, because the dots (codes) really are connected. It is the links between memory codes that form the structure of memory.

For example, consider the concept 'cat'. There is quite a lot of information in my head about cats. In the picture below I have selected just a few BITS of information to give the flavour of memory codes and how they are linked.

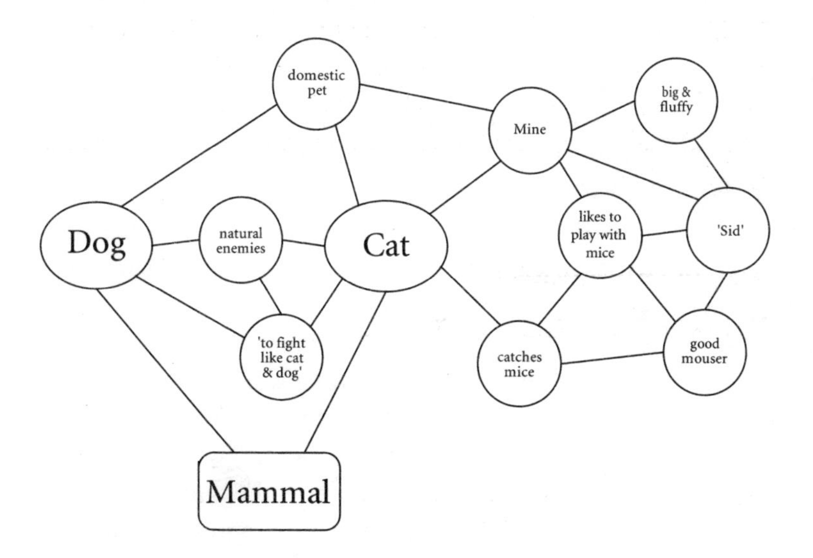

A memory code is a microcosm of memory. What we call 'memory' is a NETWORK of linked memory codes. But a memory code is itself made up of a number of bits, each of which encodes one piece of information. For example, the memory code for 'cat' includes such bits as 'catches mice' and 'domestic pet'. A memory code is therefore also a network.

The domino principle

Clearly the boundaries between memory codes are fuzzy: see how my memory code for my own cat merges in with my memory code for the more abstract 'cat' concept; the memory code for dog shares some bits with the memory code for cat. Drawing a circle around a bunch of memory bits and labelling it a particular code is to some extent an arbitrary action.

When a particular memory bit is ACTIVATED, the activation spreads along the links that bit has. The bits that belong to the same memory code will usually be very strongly linked to each other, therefore when one part of a memory code is activated, the whole code is triggered. Other memory codes will be directly linked to that memory code too (as 'dog' is to 'cat' in the example). Depending on the strength of those links, they too will be activated.

This is a fundamental principle of memory and of thought: the DOMINO PRINCIPLE. If one memory code is activated, many other codes will also become ACTIVE.

It's not necessary for links to be physically close. When we talk of links being 'close' or 'distant' we are speaking metaphorically. Even the bits of a code need not be physically close to each other.

Memory is a tightly bound, loosely woven net. The shape of your memory comes from what you've bound tightly, and what is connected only loosely. You create the coded representations held in your memory, and you choose their place in the net.

2 Finding memories

'Remembering' can be separated into two main processes: putting information in, and getting information out. *Putting information in* involves changing the information into a memory code, hence the term ENCODING. *Getting the information out* is known as RETRIEVING.

Encoding and retrieving are two sides of the same coin. How we think the information will be retrieved will affect how it is encoded. (We saw that in my experience with the letters and the library book.) Furthermore, the way in which information is encoded affects how easily the information can be retrieved.

For example, we've all had the experience of not being able to name a familiar face seen in the 'wrong' place. Maybe it's the attendant at your local petrol station. However often you see him, if you never see him anywhere but at the petrol station you will almost certainly find it difficult to remember who he is if you see him in the 'wrong' place. And the more different the place is from the usual CONTEXT, the harder it will be to retrieve the needed information. So if you see him at the shops near the petrol station, it might only take you a moment to make the connection, but if you see him in a completely unexpected place, say when you are on holiday in a distant town, it may take you hours or even days (perhaps not until you see him again in his usual place).

This occurs because the information about the particular

person (*local petrol station attendant*) is encoded under a particular location (*local petrol station*). *Local petrol station* will trigger *local petrol station attendant* fastest; *local* will probably soon trigger *local petrol station,* and similarly *petrol station* will soon trigger *local petrol station.* but if you can't find a code that will eventually lead to *local petrol station*, then you won't 'remember' whose familiar face you saw.

On the other hand, if the attendant also belonged to your tennis club, your memory code for the actual person will be more individual: not just *local petrol station attendant*, but *Tom who works at the petrol station and belongs to my tennis club*. In this case, your memory code is different; not so dominated by place or function. You are far more likely to recognise him out of context.

If you want to reliably recognise someone whom you consistently meet in one particular context you need to create a memory code that gives due weight to individual characteristics.

You create and re-create your memory. If you don't find what you're looking for, if you can't 'remember', then the reason lies in how you have constructed the memory code.

How memories are retrieved

Memories are codes that shift and change as new information comes in, as our perspective and opinions change. Memories are not cast in stone; they are written in sand. But we can follow tracks in the sand.

'Remembering' is about finding a particular memory code in the complex network of codes that is memory. To find a code, we follow a trail.

For example, think of the petrol station attendant seen on holiday. If you wanted to retrieve the identity of this annoyingly familiar face, you would try and track it down by asking yourself a number of questions:

Have I seen this person recently? Yes

Do I see this person regularly? Yes

To do with work? No

To do with children? No

Lives nearby? No

Service person? Yes

Librarian? No

Supermarket checkout? No

Petrol station? Yes!

An effective search follows a good trail, And a good trail needs a good starting point.

Recall cues

You could of course have gone completely off the rails by answering yes to, say, the question whether the person had some connection with your children. The questions which define our trail, the bits of information that prompt our recall, are called RETRIEVAL OR RECALL CUES, and your success at remembering is wholly dependent on how good they are.

If you had decided the person had something to do with your children you would have followed a different trail. Retrieval cues signpost the trails. Successful retrieval hinges on good recall cues.

Imagine that you have been asked to name as many countries as you can. You would probably start with your own country, then move on to your country's closest neighbours. After that, it gets more problematic. Initially you might keep with the geographical association and simply move around the globe, but because countries are not lined up neatly, at some point you're going to change tack. The strategy you are most likely to come up with is using continental labels as recall cues.

The order in which you go through these reveals which recall cues are strongest: which continents you are most familiar with. But a number of countries are not clearly part of any continental grouping. To recall these you need different cues. For example, 'islands: Pacific'. Some countries will be part of a continent, but their association with that continent may be very weak. You might think of Iran primarily in terms of its religious leaders, not as a country of Asia. If someone said 'pyramid' to you, no doubt Egypt would immediately spring to mind, but it might well be overlooked if you're looking for countries of Africa. The key to a successful search is finding the right signpost.

Exercise 2.1

Read carefully through the following list of 28 words twice, then shut the book and write down on a piece of paper as many words as you can remember, in any order.

> rose, pineapple, tights, sofa, archery, truck, ape, pomegranate, dress, tennis, gondola, crocus, vanity, gazelle, trousers, banana, bus, table, sailing, fox, daisy, hat, cabinet, scooter, softball, squirrel, mango, hyacinth.

These 28 words belong to seven different catgories: flowers, fruit, clothing, furniture, sport, vehicles and mammals. On another piece of paper, write down these category labels. Now see how many words you can recall under each label. Compare this with the number of words you recalled earlier.

Most people find that the category cues improve their recall.

What makes an effective signpost?

I'm afraid there is no rule that governs this. Although memory trainers tend to focus on the straightforward advice that recall cues should be funny or bizarre or rhyming, the question of whether a recall cue is effective is not quite that simple. Any memory code can be an effective recall cue. The effectiveness of a recall cue is measured by its results.

An effective recall cue leads, fairly easily, to the TARGET memory code. The category label *vehicle* is a perfectly adequate cue for *bus* or *truck*, because they are examples of the category that come very readily to mind. *Gondola*, on the other hand, is not likely to be readily accessed from *vehicle*, although it clearly does belong to the category. An effective recall cue begins a path to the target that is short and well travelled.

Sometimes we are handed the perfect recall cue on a plate, but this is a matter of good fortune. Much of the time our target memory code will not be directly linked to our first recall cue. Instead we will be required to follow a trail of linked codes. The first cue will activate codes directly linked to it, and they in turn will activate those codes linked to them. The memory codes that act as triggers or prompts – the codes between the first recall cue and the target code – are known as SECONDARY RECALL CUES.

You can of course simply play the association game and be a passive spectator while codes trigger others in a way that reflects the structure of memory. However, while this can be entertaining, it is not a particularly effective way to search for a specific memory.

A far more effective way of searching is to *actively* generate recall cues (GENERATION STRATEGY). For example, a person trying to recall members of a familiar category, such as foods, will remember more if they can generate category members that might work as additional recall cues. You might start by thinking 'fruit', which would act as a secondary recall cue. When you had run out of fruit, you might move on to 'vegetables', and so on.

You will usually have a better memory for items that you have generated yourself compared to items that have been presented to you, probably because they have more meaning for you. Your skill at generating secondary recall cues is critical in deciding whether or not you will find the target information. The basic principle underlying an effective generation strategy is that potential targets are generated in a systematic fashion that prevents the person from generating the same concepts again and again.

Exercise 2.2

1. Your insurance company has just rung to say that your insurance has lapsed because you haven't paid the bill. Your chequebook assures you that you made out a cheque three days ago, but you can't remember posting it. What recall cues might prompt your memory?

2. You see a familiar face at the supermarket, but can't remember where you know the person from. What recall cues might prompt your memory?

3. You see a person you know – you remember that she belongs to your tennis club – but you cannot remember her name. What recall cues might prompt your memory?

Context

If the key to a successful search is finding the right signpost, the question becomes: How do we know which is the right signpost?

Which trail you select – which signpost you think is correct – depends a great deal on context. Context guides the direction of your thoughts.

The information that you find interesting or relevant on one occasion is not necessarily the same information that you judge as worth encoding an another occasion. The information that is emphasised on one occasion is not necessarily stressed on another occasion. Context determines how you experience and encode information. Accordingly, context is a major factor in determining how closely linked your memory code for an experience is to a particular retrieval cue.

For example, if you went to a concert and the most important parts of the experience to you were that your friend made you so late you missed the first half-hour, that you ended up standing by the door because the seats were so bad, and that you had missed a really great programme on TV because of this awful experience, you're not likely to remember it two years later when your friend says, 'Do you remember that time we were at a concert and we ran into that woman from Telecom during the interval?' Assuming you had been to a number of concerts together, this is not likely to be a great cue. On the other hand, if your friend says, 'Remember that concert we were so late for? You were so-o grumpy!', that is much more likely to do the trick.

Every experience contains a wealth of information from which we choose the bits that will be used as a basis for encoding. Context sets us up to pay more attention to some aspects rather than others. Even mood, our own emotional state, is part of the context. So is the physical environment.

For example, in one rather dramatic experiment, scuba divers learned a list of 40 words either on a beach or ten feet underwater.

When asked to recall the words, those divers who were tested in the place in which they had studied the material did better than those who were tested in the other location.

In most everyday situations we have little control over the major contextual factors surrounding the information we are encoding or trying to find. However, in more formal learning situations, there is a greater potential to control some of these factors (see studying for an exam, page 97).

What really determines the difficulty of recall is the degree to which the encoding and retrieval contexts match (the CONTEXT EFFECT). If encoding occurs in more than one context, the chance is greater that the context when retrieving will be similar. The greater the number of encoding contexts, the greater the chance of the retrieval context being similar.

Context is a two-edged sword. The more the retrieval context is like the context at the time of encoding, the more likely it is that appropriate recall cues will be triggered, because the trail you follow is more likely to be in the correct direction. However, the retrieval context, by being unlike the encoding context, can mislead you as to the right trail to follow. The less the retrieval context matches the encoding context, the more important your skill at generating cues.

Faces and context

Faces are strongly connected to context. When we try to remember who someone is, our first thought is almost invariably, *where* do I know them from? A person whom you only see in one particular place is remembered more easily (but only in that place).

In one study that looked at face recognition in everyday life, one participant believed for a long time that a person she saw in two different places was actually two different people!

Context, then, is important for two main reasons:

- Context influences the meaning placed on the selected information, and hence how it is encoded.
- Context also may be encoded *with* the selected material, and provide additional retrieval cues.

Goals

We need a guide because a) trails can be quite long, and b) there are so many trails.

While contextual information guides your search, you need something else to help you assess whether the trail you are following is likely to lead you to the target. The information that you use to assess your choice of trial is the same information you use to judge whether you've reached your target. That information is contained in your GOAL.

It is your goal that keeps you 'on target', keeps you from getting sidetracked, helps you decide whether or not you've gone far enough down a particular trail, helps you choose between trails, and tells you when you've reached the target. It is therefore vitally important that you have clearly specified your goal.

In most cases, this is not a problem. We usually know what we're trying to do. Sometimes, however, although we may think we know what we are doing, the goal is fuzzy. If you find a search is becoming more complicated and confusing as you pursue it, the chances are that you need to clarify your goal.

The goal has something to do with the target, and something to do with the starting point (initial recall cue), but it is also something more. Say you heard a trumpet, and the trumpet called to mind a memory of someone singing, and you initiated a search to find out who it was. The trumpet is the initial recall cue; Ella Fitzgerald (though you don't know it at that point) is the target; the goal could be specified as 'a singer I associate with a trumpet', or 'a black woman singing along with a famous black jazz trumpeter', or 'a black woman singing *They can't take that away from me* with a famous black jazz trumpeter'. How specific the goal is depends on how much information is triggered by the initial cue.

The more specific a goal is, the better a guide it will be. Part of the reason for this is that the more specific the goal is, the more information you will have about the target, and therefore the more secondary recall cues you will be able to generate.

Exercise 2.3

1. Goal: to remember whether you've posted a cheque for the car insurance. List the recall cues contained in that statement.
2. Goal: to remember whether you posted a cheque for the car insurance with the cheque to the plumber on Monday. List the recall cues contained in that statement.
3. Goal: to remember whether you posted the cheque for the car insurance with the cheque to the plumber at the corner postbox when you walked down after tea on Monday. List the recall cues contained in that statement.

Which goal is most likely to result in you recalling whether or not you posted the cheque?

Retrieval strategies

Retrieval strategies are all based on the general principle of systematically generating secondary recall cues. One common strategy is ALPHABET SEARCH. In this you try to retrieve a word or name by going through the alphabet to see if any letter triggers any memories. The advantage of this method is that the alphabet provides a foolproof way of ensuring that the potential cues are generated systematically.

To demonstrate the effectiveness of this strategy, look at the following list of countries, covering up the initial letters of the capital cities. Check off those countries for which you immediately know the capital, and check off those for which you are sure you do *not* know the capital. Now, for the remaining items, go systematically through the alphabet looking for the initial letter of the capital city. When you come to a letter that sounds right, write it down, and see if it triggers the name of the capital.

	COUNTRY	FIRST LETTER OF CAPITAL CITY
1	Albania	T
2	Belgium	B
3	Chile	S
4	Denmark	C
5	Ecuador	Q
6	Fiji	S
7	Ghana	A
8	Hungary	B
9	Iraq	B
10	Jamaica	K
11	Kenya	N
12	Lebanon	B
13	Mongolia	U
14	Nigeria	L
15	Oman	M
16	Pakistan	I
17	Syria	D
18	Taiwan	T
19	Uruguay	M
20	Vietnam	H

Now uncover the initial letters and see how many of the remaining capital cities you can recall.

Another common retrieval strategy is that of trying to place a person or an event in time or space. This strategy lacks the formal structure that enables alphabet search to so easily ensure that cues are generated systematically, but a search through time or space does provide constraints that help ensure that cues are neither repeated nor omitted.

If you can remember where you usually see a person or where you have met them before, then you stand a very good chance of retrieving the appropriate memory.

To try to place them, you need to generate possible contexts: the supermarket? the office? the library? the petrol station? your child's music group? school? friends? And so on. You will start with what seems to you to be the most probable places, and then, if necessary, move out to increasingly less probable ones.

However, you need to ensure that cues are generated systematically; you need a rule or structure to guide you. A hierarchical category structure can be useful. For example, when searching for the identity of a person, you might develop the following guiding structure:

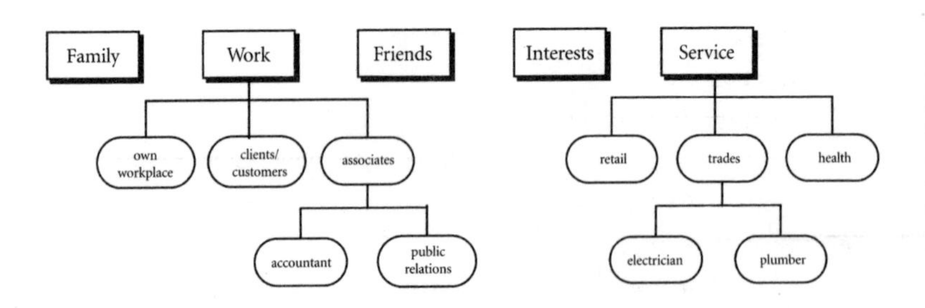

This structure is of course emblematic rather than exhaustive: to specify all the types of people you are likely to know would require more space than I have available. You would find it a useful exercise, however, to create your own, rather more specific structure. It's not necessary to go down to the ultimate level of individuals. If you specify the first two levels of your search structure, and in such a way that its organisation seems natural to you, you will have created a structure that can guide any future identity search. It will be effective to the extent that it is a) systematic (prevents you repeating dead ends), and b) exhaustive (if you have 'service: health' as a cue, you are unlikely to forget your physiotherapist, but if the category doesn't appear in your search structure, you might well do so).

There appears to be a limit to how many responses can be made to any one cue. An effective generation strategy is, therefore, one that generates many cues.

It's on the tip of my tongue

Research suggests that we experience mental blocks (knowing we know something but not able to access it) when we are trying to retrieve information that has not been used for a long time but that we once knew well. This explains why we suffer more memory blocks as we get older: not because our memory is getting poorer, but because we have more and more information stored away that hasn't been activated for some time.

Although memories that are blocked often seem to come to mind spontaneously hours or even days later, research suggests that you only succeed in retrieving the memory if you keep trying.

If a memory is blocked, you should first use the retrieval strategies to try to generate an appropriate recall cue. If after a minute or so the memory is still blocked, the best thing to do is nothing – let it go. Do something else. After an hour or more, try again.

3 Making memories that will be easy to find

Why is it (probably) so much easier to remember that Paris is the capital of France, than it is to remember that Damascus is the capital of Syria? The obvious answer is REPETITION: you've probably heard or read the first two paired together far more often than the second pairing. But it's not quite as simple as that. Think of Damascus, Syria versus Santiago, Chile. Which is more ACCESSIBLE to you depends entirely on your own experience, but one advantage Damascus will have for many people is its link to the Bible, and to the phrase 'road to Damascus'. In other words, for many people, Damascus will have more associations connected to it than Santiago does.

Being able to remember things more easily is not simply about learning more effective retrieval strategies. First and foremost, better remembering is about better encoding. If you want to improve your memory, you need to improve your skill at making memories that are easy to find.

To find a target memory code, we need to be given or to generate a code that is closely linked to the target. Clearly the more trails that lead to the target, the greater our chances of finding an effective trail. However, there is a problem with this simple rule. All roads may lead to Rome (even via Damascus!), but if you were heading for Venice *from* Rome, would that help you find the right road? On the contrary, the many roads leading *into* the city would only make it harder to find one particular road *out* of the city.

In a network of memory codes, the code that you're trying to access has links to several memory codes, but each of these trigger memory codes also has links with other memory codes. The number of these links varies from code to code. If a memory code that only links to the target code is activated, you will easily access the target. If, on the other hand, a code with several links is activated, you have a much smaller chance of following the right trail.

The more potential cues a memory code has (the more codes that are linked to it), the more likely you are to find it, but the more links a cue has, the harder it is to find thc right link. A memory code needs to be strongly linked to a cue that has few other strong links in order to be easily found. The reason that not very much work has been done in designing effective retrieval strategies is because the key to retrieving your memories lies in the way you encoded them.

Making strong links

An effective memory code is one that is accessible. Our lives are full of the same events, the same people, the same routines. We use our memories constantly and yet for the most part we are unaware of it. Memory codes we use frequently are readily accessible, because we use them frequently. A memory code that is accessed often develops strong links. Every time a link is used it becomes stronger. This is why our minds develop 'ruts' – trails that we can't seem to help following even though we have no particular need to.

The strength of a link is also a function of how long ago it was last used. Even a link that has been used frequently at one time becomes a little rusty if it has not been used for a long while. Similarly, even if a link has only been used once or twice, if it was activated a mere five minutes ago you are unlikely to have any trouble finding it.

Of course the accessibility of a code is not only a function of its strength. After all, we have a great many memory codes that are readily available. If strength of the memory code is all that is important, why don't I ever get confused between my fridge and my sofa? Why do I never call my son by the name of our pet rabbit?

I do, however, sometimes call one son by the name of the other, and I do sometimes call our new rabbit by the name of our previous one. Why are some codes triggered by mistake for others, and why are some codes never confused? Clearly it is a matter of the match between the code and the retrieval cue. A code readily comes to mind when two factors combine: the code has strong links, and the retrieval cue matches part of the code.

The accessibility of a memory code is determined by:

- The FREQUENCY EFFECT
  The more often a code has been retrieved, the easier it becomes to find.

- The RECENCY EFFECT
  A recently retrieved code will be more easily found.

- The PRIMING EFFECT
  A code will be more easily found if linked codes have just been retrieved.

- The MATCHING EFFECT
  A code will be more easily found the more the retrieval cue matches the code.

To make a new memory code accessible, therefore, you need to link it with existing codes that are appropriate (where you would look first) and strong (frequently accessed, therefore easily found). The better your linking (more appropriate links, stronger codes, a greater number of strong codes), the more easily you will find that new encoded memory.

For example, to remember the priming effect – its name and meaning – you should link it not only with the other principles of accessibility, but also with information that is already familiar to you and which adds meaning to the new information. There are several, related, uses of the term 'to prime' which are relevant to its use in this context: to prime the pump; to prime a firearm; to prime a person. In all cases, the meaning is to prepare something or someone so that they are ready for a particular situation.

The priming effect is meaningfully connected to another principle we have looked at earlier: the domino principle. It is also strongly connected with the recency effect. If you link the principles that codes trigger other codes (domino effect), and that codes are more easily found when they have been recently retrieved (recency effect), with the definition of priming as to prepare for use, then the priming effect (that a code is primed for activation by the recent activation of other linked codes) is readily understood and remembered.

But even better is to link the principle with a familiar experience. Think, for example, of how readily you recognise a face you have just seen. Have you noticed that recognising is even easier if you see the face from the same angle, with the same expression? Have you noticed that recognition is *not* helped by recently seeing the *name* – but it *is* helped by seeing an associated face, such as that of a child or sibling? To make new codes accessible, link them meaningfully to existing strong codes.

Improving memory codes

All this talk of making and strengthening links between codes sounds very technical, as if these are complex strategies. But of course, whether we are conscious of it or not, we are doing this all the time, constantly. To remember, to observe, to reflect, to learn – all are processes that involve the making and strengthening of codes and the links between them.

Repetition – and spacing

To say that links are stronger if they are frequently activated is to make explicit the principle beneath the most common memory strategy of all – so common that we don't even need to be taught it: repetition.

Although we all know that repetition is important to memory, few of us appreciate the power of even a single repetition. For example, one study found that when people were briefly shown random words to learn, they remembered on average only about 27 per cent of words that appeared once compared to 46 per cent of words that appeared twice.

Repetition is much more effective if repetitions are separated from each other by other pieces of information. Most of the advantage of spacing occurs with as little as two intervening items between repetitions, but this advantage continues to increase as the interval increases (SPACING EFFECT). The most effective strategy, in fact, is to repeat at increasingly long intervals.

The spacing effect probably occurs for the same reason that learning something in different contexts increases the likelihood and speed of retrieving the memory: there are more potential retrieval cues. The spacing effect therefore is linked to the context effect and the matching effect.

The effectiveness of spaced repetitions is also partly that, when repetitions are presented closely together, people tend not to pay much attention to the repetition. But they pay *more* attention to later presentations when the presentations are more distant. This agrees with common sense – most of us would feel that we wouldn't pay much attention to a word being repeated over and over again, but that if we were learning a list and an item cropped up again some time after its first presentation, we would notice it particularly.

Because the spacing effect is a variant of the context effect, you can compensate for a lack of time between repetitions by taking measures to create a change in context. In other words, if you can't space your study of particular material over time, you should try and change the context; either physically (by changing your environment) or by trying to change your mental perspective (much harder).

Clustering

Making an effective (accessible) memory code involves appropriately connecting the code to existing codes. Effective encoding is therefore about CLUSTERING.

When people are asked to recall specific events that have happened to them, they typically cluster events around a particular THEME. Here are two examples of how someone recalled events that had happened to him (from a study by Barsalou).

First, in terms of a particular activity (swimming):

- went swimming at Red Oaks with a friend of mine
- went swimming at the University of Hartford because my brother went to summer school there
- went to the reservoir.

Second, in terms of a specific event (going to 'Circus World' one day):

- my brother ... brought his girlfriend ... I brought my boyfriend . . . my mum and dad went
- it was really good
- we rode all sorts of rides
- we saw a circus
- we spent most of the day there.

Event clusters can also be organised by time, or place, or the people involved.

In general, items are clustered together by virtue of the connections between them, by virtue of sharing attributes. The connections between items give meaning to them, but meaning also – and to a greater extent – derives from a theme. A meaningful cluster has a theme that unites the components that belong to it. The theme is the glue that holds the cluster together.

For example, if a friend tells you they've bought a new car and it's a Toyota Corolla, you will probably have little trouble remembering the fact of the new car. However, if you have no particular interest in cars, and no special knowledge of that make of car, you are likely to forget that it is a Toyota Corolla. On the other hand, if you know someone else with a Toyota Corolla, this will provide an additional link which will increase your likelihood of remembering. If *two* of your friends have that make of car, you will have two links, and your chances of remembering will be even greater.

But what if a third friend acquires a Toyota Corolla? Now the ownership of this particular make of car becomes an item of more interest. Suddenly realising that *three* of your friends own a Toyota

Corolla, you form links between those memory codes. Ownership of a Toyota Corolla has become more meaningful.

If another piece of information was linked to these codes (maybe something you recently read about this make of car, or your own need to replace your car), then the significance of 'Toyota Corolla' would become even greater, and the connected codes may become thematically linked. They become a cluster.

In the same way, in the supermarket, tinned vegetables are grouped together, fruit and vegetables, dairy products, frozen foods. But not all items so clearly belong to a particular group. Personally, I never know where to find maple syrup, because, although I would group it with golden syrup, treacle, molasses, etc., my supermarket puts it with ice-cream toppings. This makes no sense to me because I never put maple syrup on ice cream.

This brings us to the first principle of effective clustering:

1. Cluster information in a way that makes sense *to you*

This doesn't mean that you have to do it yourself. Although you probably intuitively feel that if you organise information yourself, you will remember it better than if someone else organises it for you, this does not seem to be true. The important thing is that the clustering *makes sense* to you, not who does it.

The way you cluster information makes a huge difference to the way you encode it, and to the likelihood of you retrieving it. This is true even in such an apparently straightforward case as remembering a telephone number. If someone tells you their phone number with a pause after each group of two or three or four digits, this will encourage you to CHUNK the digits in that way (and is more effective than if the digits are spoken evenly). But if the person then repeats the number, this will help your recall *only if the pauses are in the same place.*

In other words, 528 3467 is a completely different number from 52 83 467. (How often has someone spoken your own phone number to you, and you have had to repeat it back with your own grouping before you can verify its accuracy?)

Themes integrate clusters and labels articulate the themes. Think of the way supermarket aisles are labelled with the categories of items stored there. These labels may be considered as the themes that encapsulate the important shared attribute of the members of the group. To the extent that the labels do successfully encapsulate that common attribute, the labelling will be successful. But of course, as we all know from personal experience, the labels are not always successful.

Why not? Because the supermarket understandably wants to limit the number of category labels on the signs, and the broader your category, the less likely it is that all members of that category will clearly and unambiguously share one common attribute. To be able to label a cluster effectively, the cluster needs to be narrowly focused.

2. Only include information that is tightly linked in the same cluster

This is the criterion: can you come up with a word or brief phrase that applies to each of the bits of information within the cluster? If not, the cluster is not sufficiently tightly linked. It contains information that doesn't belong.

The more specific the theme is, the better. The degree to which the codes in a cluster are connected to each other is reflected in the specificity of the theme.

Look at the following set of statements (taken from a study by Cantor and Engle):

- The teacher took a table near a window.
- The teacher read the menu.

- The teacher asked for a glass of water.
- The teacher checked his wallet.
- The teacher munched on a breadstick.
- The teacher placed an order.

Compare these statements with the following set:

- The teacher took a table near a window.
- The teacher read the menu.
- The teacher found that the prices were high.
- The teacher checked his wallet.
- The teacher decided he could afford a steak.
- The teacher placed an order.

Both sets of statements may be regarded as being related by a theme: having a meal at a restaurant. But the two different sentences in the second set increase the integration of the statements dramatically. This increase in the number and strength of the connections between the statements of the set is reflected in the more specific theme of the second set: the cost of going out for a meal.

If you learned the information in these two sets of statements, and were then asked questions about them, you would take longer to retrieve information from the first set of statements. If more statements were added to the sets, it would take even longer, because each statement would need to be activated and checked (the FAN EFFECT). However, retrieving information from the second set of statements would not be slowed by the number of statements in the set, as long as the statements were tightly linked. In other words, although codes take longer to retrieve the greater the number of linked codes they have, codes in a cluster take no longer to retrieve regardless of the number of codes in the cluster.

3. More, smaller clusters are better than fewer, larger clusters

People tend to recall about the same number of items from a cluster (about five). It's a good idea therefore to break information into more clusters rather than fewer. For example, if you had 40 items to remember, around 25 items would be remembered if you learned them as five groups of eight items, but all of them might be remembered if you had put them into eight groups of five.

4. Give each cluster a unique identifying label

The clusters serve as secondary recall cues. This is why, to be effective, they need some sort of identifying label. This label usually encapsulates the theme. The label *anchors* the codes in a cluster. Go back to our supermarket example: whether you have a physical or mental shopping list, it helps to have an awareness that you want vegetables, fruit, meat, dairy, frozen goods, and something from personal toiletries.

5. Connect related clusters

Clustering on its own only helps to connect the information within a cluster, so we also need to connect the clusters. One cluster must lead to another. Thus, if you have a list of 40 items to learn and you have divided it into eight clusters of five, you would ideally like any one of those eight labels (retrieval cues) to trigger all other clusters. If, indeed, you managed to build strong connections between *all* the clusters, you would have built a super-cluster.

Say you write down your supermarket items during the week as you think of them:

broccoli	shampoo	soap	oranges
apples	kidney beans	tacos	frozen beans
cheese	icing sugar	chicken nuggets	yeast
frozen peas	cabbage	red peppers	rice
quick noodles	yogurt	fresh soya milk	kiwi fruit
eggs	tinned fruit	cornflakes	pasta
toilet paper	tissues	washing powder	fruit juice
tomatoes	hash browns	margarine	strawberry jam
rice flakes	courgettes	bananas	bread
frozen blueberries	bacon	caster sugar	pears

These fall (rather more neatly than usual!) into eight categories of five – *my* eight categories, that is. Why don't you see what categories you get? My answers (and there's no 'right' answer; what's important is what makes sense to you) are at the end of the book.

So now you have a number of clusters, and in one sense they

already belong to a super-cluster (the supermarket shopping list cluster). But you can strengthen the links between the clusters by connecting them. My standard way is in terms of supermarket layout (so vegetables come first, then fruit, because people enter my supermarket through this area).

6. Make as many links between clusters as you can

The more connections we can make between different clusters, the more integrated the network of clusters, and the more meaningful the information will be. Remember, it is the connections between information that give it meaning. And it is the connections – their number and strength – that make memory codes accessible.

A super-cluster has many potential retrieval cues. Information in a super-cluster is readily accessible and a super-cluster is treated as a single item. This is why the fan effect (slow retrieval when too many paths lead into and out of the memory code) doesn't apply to codes in a super-cluster.

Why does an expert learn new information so easily?

One of the characteristics of experts is that they can acquire new information in their subject much more easily than a novice. The reason for this is that an expert has a strong framework – a tightly linked network of super-clusters.

Moreover, an expert's clusters and super-clusters usually have deeper anchors. Typically, a novice clusters information on the basis of superficial similarities, whereas an expert builds clusters around meaningful principles and relationships.

Patterns

It is well accepted that organising information in a hierarchical or linear arrangement improves recall, but organising information in a matrix can be even more effective. Compare the following examples showing items organised in (a) a hierarchical arrangement, and (b) a matrix structure (example taken from a study by Broadbent, Cooper and Broadbent):

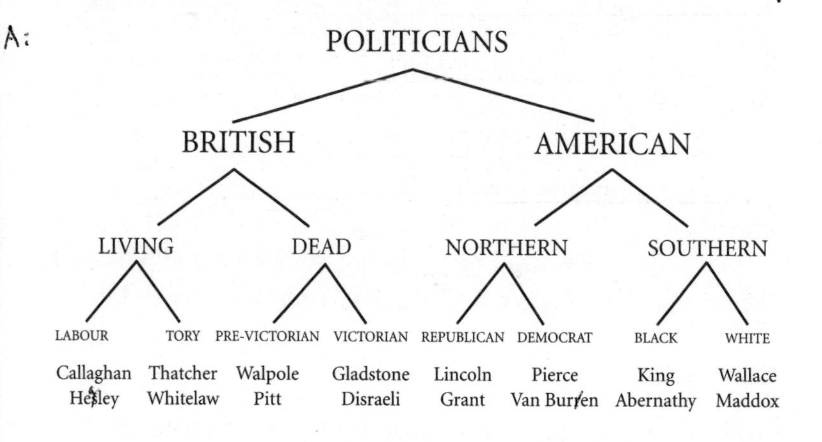

POLITICIANS

	BEFORE 1900		AFTER 1900	
	BRITISH	AMERICAN	BRITISH	AMERICAN
A–L	Gladstone Disraeli	Lincoln Grant	Callaghan Healey	King Abernathy
M–Z	Walpole Pitt	Pierce Van Buren	Thatcher Whitelaw	Wallace Maddox

Both these ways of organising information dramatically improve recall compared to a mere list of items, but the matrix arrangement has an advantage in that there are more retrieval paths to the items. Thus, for example, if you forgot the retrieval cue TORY (in the hierarchical arrangement), you would be unable to access Thatcher and Whitelaw. But if you forgot the cue M–Z, you might still access Thatcher and Whitelaw through BRITISH.

Reflecting the greater number of retrieval paths, a matrix also demonstrates more connections than a hierarchical structure. If you study the names of politicians in the hierarchical tree, the only items that are transparently linked are the paired names. However, if you study the matrix, the connections between, say, Gladstone and Disraeli, and Walpole and Pitt, are very obvious.

The key to memory lies in setting up good retrieval cues. The important question thus becomes, not 'How do I get a good memory?', but 'How can I best organise this material to provide a rich set of potential recall cues so that it is easy to remember?'

Exercise 3.1

Here is a set of statements about the life of Antonio Vivaldi, composer of the *Four Seasons*:

Birth
1. He was born in Venice in 1678, on the day of an earthquake.
2. He was the eldest of eight children, and the only one to become a musician.

Parent
3. His father was a professional violinist.

Job
4. He was ordained a priest in 1703.
5. His first official post was as a violin master.

Physical
6. He had red hair, and was nicknamed 'the red priest'.

7. He ceased to say Mass not long after his ordination.

8. He lost part of his income through his failure to say Mass.

9. He blamed his failure to say Mass on an ailment he had suffered from childhood (possibly asthma).

10. In 1737 he was censured for conduct unbecoming to a priest.

11. He was refused entry to Ferrara on the grounds of his supposed relationship with a singer and his refusal to say Mass.

12. Although he had composed many pieces, which had been very popular and well paid, he died in poverty.

Which of these statements are connected? Can you form any clusters, where each statement is connected with every other statement, and whose shared connections can be encapsulated in a single theme? What is the theme (in a word or phrase)?

Now close the book and see how many statements you can recall (for meaning, not verbatim). You should find that statements you have linked with others are easier to recall than isolated statements, and that clustered statements are much easier to recall.

4 Choosing what to remember

We are all familiar with the way distinctive smells can trigger particular memories. For example, I always remember my grandmother when I smell Christmas lilies, because whenever we arrived for Christmas at her house she would have them arranged on the hall table, and their distinctive fragrance would fill the hall.

Smell is not unique in its power to evoke memories. In fact, smell works in the same way as any other cue. Like any contextual cue, information learned in the presence of a novel smell is remembered better if the smell is available during retrieval. If the smell is a familiar one, a smell that's odd for the context is a better recall cue than an appropriate one.

We choose what to remember, and what we choose depends on what we notice. We're far more likely to notice something that stands out, for whatever reason.

Aim for the distinctive

Memory codes are selected bits of information. The links that connect a code with other codes – and consequently the retrieval cues that will be effective – depend on what bits of information have been selected.

Much of the reason that some people have a 'good' memory and others have a 'bad' one lies in the different ways people encode information. What aspects are selected for encoding? What aspects are rejected? What governs the selection?

One important rule guiding our selection is that we look for features that are shared by as few other items as possible (the DISTINCTIVENESS PRINCIPLE). This is in keeping with our principle of choosing effective retrieval cues (an effective retrieval cue contains information that is matched by few other codes in your network). The selection of these distinctive features is guided by context.

For example, the image of a girl doing a handstand would be distinctive in an advertisement for office furniture, but unremarkable in the context of a gymnastics display. If the girl was dressed in a suit, this would be distinctive whatever the context, but if the viewer's own small child was also in the scene this might well overwhelm even such a bizarre sight as a girl in a suit doing a handstand. In other words, distinctiveness is not only relative, but also subjective.

You can reduce distinctiveness by concentrating on some highly general information. For example, in a list of words you could focus on the number of 'e's. In such circumstances you are less likely to notice any distinctive words (such as *computer* among a list of fruits). However, if the word is structurally distinctive (*phlegm*, for example, has an unusual sequence of letters giving it a distinctive 'shape'), it is likely to be more easily remembered in a situation where you are concentrating on some very general aspect.

Similarly, distinctiveness is increased, and therefore your chance of remembering, when you focus on an aspect of an item that distinguishes it from the surrounding items. For example, in a list of fruit *banana* is not likely to stand out. However, if you are specifically picking out fruit that start with 'b', *banana* will be more distinctive.

Make codes specific

If *banana* is encoded simply as a common fruit, then it will be harder to find among all the other common fruit than if it is coded under *common fruit that start with 'b'*. If it is coded as *common fruit that starts with 'b' and is yellow* it will be even easier to find. When encoding an item you need enough information to distinguish that item from all the other items already stored. The more specific the code, the more quickly and easily it will be found.

Hence, if you're trying to think of the name of a fruit, you will get on better if you know its starting letter, better still if you remember that it repeated itself, and best of all if you remember it had something to do with a cat's foot (pawpaw!). The important thing is to find distinctive features that uniquely specify the concept. Remember, the more distinctive it is, the easier it will be to find in your memory.

Use fragments

Essentially you are looking for features (bits of a code) that will be good retrieval cues. These may even be fragments of an item.

Say you wanted to remember the name of a company: *Computer Cable Services Ltd*. You might simply repeat the whole name a few times to yourself and hope that it will just pop up when you need it. But this is not particularly likely to be successful if you have not paid any special attention to the individual words. The first word, *Computer*, is too common to serve as a good recall cue, and this is the one you are likely to have paid most attention to, simply because it is first. If, however, you have marked *Cable* as the least common term in the company's name and made a special effort to remember that, you are far more likely to be successful in remembering the name. When you try to retrieve the name, if you have been successful in remembering that one word (*Cable*), a cue that is not likely to be linked with many other items, the link to *Computer Cable Services Ltd* is likely to be the most recent and consequently will be easily accessed. *Cable* has thus provided an anchor for *Computer Cable Services Ltd.*

The fragment being used as a recall cue does not need to be a whole word. For example, you might pick out *hypo* or *thyroid* to help you remember the medical term *hypothyroidism*. Which fragment will be the better recall cue depends on you and whichever you find more distinctive.

In essence, while we look for similarities to make connections, we look for differences to uniquely identify a code. Distinctive cues anchor the code.

Exercise 4.1

Look back at the details you recalled about the life of Vivaldi. Were there any details that were trivial in themselves, but that you recalled because they were unusual or interesting? Did recall of these details cue you to remembrance of more significant linked items?

Memorising versus learning

The rules are a little different when it comes to word-for-word rote memorisation, which is why we commonly distinguish between this sort of learning and 'true' learning. For most of us, memorising is a matter of brute force. The principal tool is simple repetition. You recite the information over and over and over again, until you have pounded it into your brain. It works – I can still recite a piece from *A Midsummer Night's Dream* that I learned by this method one dreary Sunday afternoon about 25 years ago – but it is hard work, and of course very boring.

Memorising is what we do when we need to remember the exact words, as in the following situations:

- memorising words from a foreign language
- memorising speeches, poems, etc.
- memorising names and faces
- memorising a shopping list
- memorising 'phone numbers.

But of course, in most situations we only need to remember the sense of the information.

True learning requires understanding, which comes from the connections between codes. In one sense it is harder work than memorisation, because you must think; you must dig for the connections. Memorisation is boring and time-consuming, but it is not difficult as such. However, true learning builds on itself. If you put the effort into understanding material you find difficult, you will reap your reward in the long term: later information will be acquired more easily. It will 'slot in' to your existing framework. Memorisation doesn't build on itself; it is just as difficult to memorise a related text as it was to memorise the first text.

Make it meaningful

In materials without inherent structure, organisation must be forced on the information. To aid recall, meaning is imposed by selecting and connecting meaningful codes to the material to be memorised. The selection of information is thus quite different for material that is not organised around a theme.

We all know that meaningless strings of words or numbers are hard to learn. Telephone numbers, for example, usually begin with digits that reflect the area the telephone is in, and go on to list digits that simply reflect when the telephone was connected. If you are familiar with the area code, then the first digits have some meaning to you and are therefore easier to remember. However the last digits appear completely random and are accordingly much more difficult to learn.

In this situation, two common strategies are used. Either we try to find some sort of pattern or meaning in the digits, or, if we only want to remember the number long enough to dial it or write it down, we continuously repeat it to ourselves. Although simple repetition is adequate when we only need to remember something for a few minutes, the information will slip away as soon as we stop repeating it.

We do of course remember phone numbers that we use frequently. This is because of the sheer number of times the information is activated (strengthening the code) and because the repetition is spaced.

Acquiring a phone number this way takes time, however. A more effective and quicker strategy is to add meaning. The use of letters on telephones to encode the digits enables phone-numbers to be transformed into words: 0800 ANSETT is much more meaningful and easier to remember than 0800 267388.

Meaningless does not mean random. While telephone numbers may be arbitrary, we cannot say that a sonnet is a random arrangement of words. The distinction I make between information that is meaningful and information that is meaningless is not a distinction between sense and nonsense, but a distinction depending on whether your goal is to understand or to parrot.

Where understanding is your goal, clustering and meaningful connections between codes is important. But where your goal is to be able to reproduce information verbatim, the emphasis is on forcing links with strong codes, to establish better retrieval cues.

The transformation of meaningless information into meaningful information (either through direct transformation or indirectly through connections with meaningful codes) is the basis of MNEMONIC STRATEGIES of all kinds (discussed at length in chapter nine). Essentially, mnemonic strategies are all about making good recall cues. So let's look at what makes good recall cues, and how you make strong connections when the information isn't meaningfully related.

Concrete words

It is well known that words that refer to concrete, easily visualised objects (like *apple*, *book*, *house*), are remembered more easily than words that refer to abstract concepts (for example, *justice*, *love*). This is because concrete words are particularly effective as recall cues.

Concrete words seem to have many more links to other codes than abstract concepts do, and, because of this wider network, concrete words are far more easily associated with otherwise meaningless material.

Easily-visualised cues

Concreteness may be defined in terms of how easy it is to form a mental image of the concept. In a situation where it is hard to produce images (for example, when words are presented very briefly and quickly, or when a person is unaware of the need to try to remember the material), the advantage of concrete words over abstract words is much less. Moreover, if people are told to form images there is no difference between the learning of abstract and concrete words. It appears then that concrete words are usually remembered better because concrete words are more easily visualised than abstract words. This rule for choosing concrete words is therefore more accurately expressed as: choose cues that are easily visualised.

Make the connection

The effectiveness of IMAGERY is well documented. One study found that forming mental images was more than twice as effective as simply repeating the material (the most basic strategy). But imagery is most effective when interacting or RELATIONAL IMAGES are used. Indeed interaction is in large part the key to the effectiveness of imagery.

For example, if you had to memorise the words: CAT DRUM BROOM TABLE, you would be better to make one image (of, say, a cat sweeping a table with a drum balanced on his head) rather than four different images.

Items may be related to one another through words as well as by images. One way of relating items verbally is by making up a story. For example, here is a brief story to help memorise a shopping list of ten items (the items are capitalised):

> The BREAD is full of JUICE. I will MILK it and watch the RICE BUBBLE away, then FISH for CORN, CHIP it into BEANS and STOCK up on ORANGES.

The use of this strategy has a dramatic effect on rote-learning, compared to the use of a simple strategy such as repetition.

Although imagery is propounded by many memory trainers as the secret to memory improvement, there is not in fact anything particularly miraculous about its use. Verbal associations can be equally effective retrieval cues. The advantage of visual images is quite simply that it is often easier to make connections between codes by visualising them together than by connecting them with words. On the other hand, many people find it difficult to create images.

The key to remembering unrelated material is in forming relationships between the concepts. This can be done through mental images, or through words. Pick which one you are more comfortable with.

Other good cues

Some words by their very nature are easier to remember than other words, and so provide particularly good recall cues:

- words that look odd (e.g. *phlegm*)
- words that sound or look similar (e.g. *sound – hound*; *foreman – human*)
- common words that are required to be pronounced in an uncommon way (e.g. *colonel, ache, one, two, knee, aisle*).

So synonyms, rhymes, words that are unusual in looks or sound, and words that are easily visualised are all potentially effective recall cues. Nor should you restrict yourself to whole words: words that contain memorable fragments are also useful.

Exercise 4.2

Look again at the list of statements about Vivaldi in the previous chapter. Pick out the details that you consider distinctive. Consider the connections you made. Can you form new links by emphasising the distinctive details?

Now see how many details you can recall about Vivaldi.

Paying attention

Encoding can occur without intention and without effort. But to encode well, you need to pay attention. If you divide your attention when encoding information, you markedly reduce your memory for that information. Dividing your attention when trying to remember has much less impact on your ability to retrieve information; retrieval is more of an automatic process than encoding. After all, retrieval simply involves following a marked trail, but encoding involves selecting the information to be encoded, and connecting it with related information.

Use the right strategy

Attention is not synonymous with effort. To say that someone works hard is not the same as saying that they work well. Working hard refers mainly to the number of hours spent, while working well refers to an outcome.

Effort alone doesn't produce good learning. We are all familiar with people who never seem to work hard at studying but do well at exams, and people who work, work, work, and still do poorly. This is not simply a matter of one being 'smarter' than the other. You can try as hard as you like, but if you are using the wrong learning strategy for a particular task, then the information will not be well encoded so will be harder to retrieve.

But you can minimise time spent by using appropriate learning strategies and applying the principles of learning. An hour of concentrated, well-directed learning is worth several hours of misdirected or poorly attended effort. Of course the trick is in knowing where to direct your attention. The essence of knowing where to focus lies in remembering and applying the fundamentals of encoding and retrieving. So, create good potential retrieval cues by selecting distinctive information and forming appropriate and strong links. The role of attention is to improve your chances of achieving these goals.

5 Different parts of memory

Information is not all the same. The information contained in a face is treated differently than the information in a textbook. A feeling of grief is remembered in a different way to the experience of going to a restaurant. This seems obvious and yet, when people talk about memory, they tend to speak of it as one thing. Memory is not a 'thing'. Memory is a process.

The memory process depends on the domain of the information. Knowing the MEMORY DOMAIN helps you distinguish different types of information and different memory tasks, and helps you recognise which strategy is appropriate.

The differences between various types of information are not always as obvious as those between, say, events and emotions, faces and facts. For example, here are two similar scenarios: a) you remember you've heard Wynton Marsalis in concert, but you can't immediately remember who accompanied you; b) you recognise a face as familiar but can't immediately remember who the person is.

The most effective strategy to find the name of the person who accompanied you to the concert is not the same strategy you should use to find the name of the familiar person. The strategies are different because a person's identity is quite different information to the identity of a person with whom you shared an experience. One relates to the domain of events, the other to the domain of personal identity.

Most of our memory falls into one of two broad types: KNOWLEDGE MEMORY and PERSONAL MEMORY.

Knowledge memory

Knowledge memory is also known as SEMANTIC memory. It contains language and 'facts' – information in its narrower, more common meaning. Your knowledge that householders pay money to the local council in return for such services as street lights, sewage reticulation, public libraries and parks, etc. is part of knowledge memory. Your knowledge that this money is called 'council tax' is part of knowledge memory. Your knowledge that you pay £60 per month council tax is part of personal memory.

People who temporarily 'lose' their memory can't access personal memory, but usually still have access to their knowledge memory. They remember the colour 'red', even though they don't remember that red was the colour of their first car. They know how to use the telephone, although they cannot remember any phone numbers.

In other words, knowledge memory contains information about the world; while personal memory contains information about *you.*

It has been suggested that within knowledge memory separate domains may exist for numbers, for music and for language. These are all types of information that appear to be dealt with in different ways.

Language

In general, knowledge memory is assumed to be organised around concepts – concepts being, as it were, the 'theme' of a category. Categories are clusters, or super-clusters. Members of a category belong by virtue of being examples of the theme. The links that connect them are their similarities to each other.

Thus, a domestic cat belongs to the category (cluster) 'cat', and to the superordinate category (super-cluster) 'mammal'. Lions, tigers, leopards, etc. also belong to the category 'cat', by virtue of being examples of 'catness' (if I may be excused this term), and share among themselves a certain similarity, based on common features.

Categories are arranged hierarchically; that is, subordinate levels are progressively less abstract, so the ultimate category from which our domestic cat descends might be considered to be the very general and quite abstract 'living creature', descending through 'animal', to 'mammal', 'carnivore', 'feline' and finally, the most specific and concrete, 'cat'.

Each of these categories has different information associated with it. Thus, if you are asked whether a cat has long ears, you would consult the specific information connected with 'cat', but if you were asked whether a cat gives birth to live young, you would find the appropriate information under 'mammal'. Accessing information under associated categories takes longer, of course, than accessing information within the target category.

If you were asked whether a cat lays eggs, it would take you even longer, as properties a category *doesn't* have are rarely explicitly listed. It's also harder to reject an instance as a member of a category when the two items belong to associated categories. For example, it takes you longer to decide that a tree is not an animal (both living) than it does to decide a brick is not an animal.

Knowing that knowledge memory is organised in categories explains why category prompts are much more useful than alphabet prompts in retrieval search. It also explains why we're more likely to think of some items than others. Typical members of a category are generally remembered more quickly and easily than less typical members (you'll think of a sparrow before you think of a heron), and smaller categories are usually searched faster than larger ones.

Knowing about categories allows us to understand more fully the effects of recency and frequency. Because an item isn't usually accessed directly, but through its category label, what counts isn't the number of times you've accessed an item, but how many times you've accessed it through that particular category label. Many items belong to more than one category (a lion is not only a cat, but also a scary predator, a star of film and TV, an inhabitant of zoos: your chance of thinking it in a particular context depends on how accessible it is *in that context*).

Knowing about categories also helps us understand the difference between experts and the rest of us. Essentially, experts have more and richer categories in their area of expertise than novices do. Expert categories are also based on deep principles, while the categories that novices have tend to emphasise surface similarities. In other words, building expertise in a subject is all about developing meaningful and richly interconnected categories.

Exercise 5.1

Give yourself ten seconds to write down all the words you can think of that start with 'n'. Now give yourself ten seconds to write down all the words you can think of that belong to the category 'fruit'.

Although there are far more words beginning with 'n' than there are fruit, nevertheless you probably wrote down more fruit than words begining with 'n'. Use your knowledge about categories to search more effectively.

Numbers

Mathematics is often called a language, and to the extent that it involves symbolic knowledge, it operates like the rest of knowledge memory. The case for giving it the status of a separate domain rests partly on the primitive sense of numeracy that preverbal infants and many animals display: an ability to judge whether there is more of a thing in one group compared to another, and an ability to roughly calculate the sum of two such groups. So we can talk about a 'number sense', but any sort of precision or complexity requires a symbolic awareness that puts numbers firmly in the language domain.

But number also has a spatial aspect, as well as a rather more primitive connection to our body (we learn to count on our fingers, and that's an instinct that's never entirely lost). The spatial aspect is reflected in the mental timeline we have, that for Westerners at least, places ever-increasing numbers on a line from left (smaller) to right (larger). Numbers, then, are encoded in several different ways.

It is thought that basic arithmetic facts (such as $3 + 4 = 7$; $2 \times 8 = 16$) are stored like any basic facts, but it's suggested that any unknown or hard-to-access fact requires recoding using your understanding of magnitude and quantity. Beyond simple facts, calculations require the involvement of WORKING MEMORY, while more complex calculations involve sequential planning (SKILL MEMORY, which we'll get to later in the chapter).

In other words, becoming skilled at basic number facts is just a matter of rote learning, and how quickly and easily you know the answer is simply a function of how much practice you've put in. Being able to 'do' maths requires not only an abstract (symbolic) understanding of number, but also practice in analysing and dissecting maths problems (the more practice, the less you'll need to rely on working memory – see the discussion on skill memory – so people with lower WORKING MEMORY CAPACITY need to put more effort into this).

Music

Like number, there is something quite primitive about our response to music. Again like number, we share this aspect with other animals, but we have used language to take it to a much more sophisticated level. Many of the same brain regions are used to process both music and language, and it does appear that people remember music in much the same way that they remember speech.

Like mathematics, but in a different way, music is also tied into skill memory, and this may be one reason that music has a peculiar power to make something more memorable. Music is both physical and conceptual.

It is suggested that music is encoded in two largely independent systems working in parallel. The first focuses on pitch, and the second on rhythm.

Pitch is organised around musical scales, each of which is centred around a central tone called the tonic. The importance of other notes in the scale depends on how closely related they are to the tonic. This tonal organisation of pitch affects how you perceive music and how well you remember it by the expectancies it creates in you as you listen.

Rhythm is encoded in terms of timing: the duration of notes and the beat (the periodicity of strong and weak beats). Timing is of course utterly crucial for music, as it also is for action sequences (skill memory). It is therefore interesting to discover that high 'intelligence' (as measured by intelligence tests) is correlated with a good ability to tap out a rhythm. Is this why music training for children has been found to improve academic performance? (Probably not alone, because music training is particularly helpful for verbal skills, but it may be a factor.)

These pitch and rhythm systems are involved in the process of encoding, but they're not part of the permanent files. The output from these systems goes (according to theory) to a 'musical lexicon', which stores all the musical phrases you've heard, and to a component linked to the lexicon that stores your emotional responses (this emotional component is of course another major reason for music's memorability). If there are words attached to the music, then this too will be (separately) encoded and filed in an associated lexicon. And finally, other information (such as where you heard the music, who was playing, who was with you, the name of the tune) will be stored in separate but linked files.

As you can see, music is a particularly complex set of codes, and this richly connected network is probably the third reason why it is so memorable.

Personal memory

Although Western culture has emphasised the need to improve knowledge memory, personal memory is at least as important, and considerably more complex. In chapter 7 I identify 13 common problem tasks (see page 86). Only two pertain to knowledge memory: remembering information you have studied, and remembering the names of things.

Personal memory contains at least four domains, two of which contain several domains of their own. Far more different strategies are required to deal with these different domains.

Memory for yourself

AUTOBIOGRAPHICAL MEMORY is the memory domain concerned with the information you have about yourself. It includes a domain that contains information such as whether or not you like ice cream, what your favourite colour is, what you think about a political party, etc. (SELF-DESCRIPTION). This domain is a major part of your sense of identity and also includes EMOTIONAL MEMORY. This type of memory can help us control our moods. We can sustain a mood by dwelling on appropriate memories, or change a mood by recalling memories that involve a contrasting emotion.

People rarely worry about their ability to remember emotions or aspects of their own identity, however. The domain of interest within autobiographical memory is the domain of events.

Event memory

There are three related domains within EVENT MEMORY:

- memory for specific events that have happened to you
- memory for general events, which tells you the broad sequence of actions in events such as going to a restaurant or going to the dentist
- a potted summary of your life, which enables you to answer such questions as 'Where did you go to school?' or 'Where were you working last year?'

These may be thought of as being connected hierarchically, with our most specific and concrete level being that of specific events, subsumed in the broader category of general events, which in turn is subordinate to the overarching category of your life history.

The entry point into the event domain is usually at the general-event level. In other words, if you want to remember the time you went to see *Star Wars*, you would first consider the general event 'going to the cinema'. Because information at this level tends to be accessed relatively often, it is usually very easy to find – so easy in fact that you probably don't even notice doing so.

The memories we have trouble finding are almost always

specific events. When did I last go to the pictures? Have I read this novel? Where did I go hiking two years ago? Who did I go to see *Sleepless in Seattle* with?

Because event memory is usually entered via the general-event level, and because the information we are searching for is usually at the specific-event level, it is worth spending a little time explaining the relationship between these two separate domains.

Let us imagine that you have gone to the circus once in your life. In such a case you would readily remember that specific occasion. If you had been twice, you would probably remember each time, but perhaps be uncertain about which visit some minor detail belonged to. However, if you had been several times to the circus, you would have developed a general SCRIPT for the experience. The separate events would have become merged into this general event, and the specific events would only be remembered if they were marked by something distinctive.

You may have some memory for the first time. You will probably have some memory for the last time. You may remember the time you were very late, or the time a child threw up on your shoes. But by and large the separate events will be lost to you. What you will *not* forget is the general experience of going to the circus – the parts of the event that are usually the same. Maybe the venue, the things on sale or the acts. Maybe a feeling of excitement, a particular smell, a sound, a time of day or a type of weather.

The more often you experience a particular type of event, the stronger your memory for that type of event, and the weaker your memory for the specific occasions. That's why it's so hard to recall the details of your trip to the supermarket two weeks ago.

Moreover, the general script is so powerful that it can lead you into being utterly convinced something happened simply because it fits into the framework of your script. Memory for events reflects what you *expect* to happen, not simply what *did* happen.

The strength of scripts is perhaps why first experiences tend to be better remembered: on the first occurrence of a new experience, you have no script available and must construct one. Subsequent experiences will be interpreted and encoded in the light of that script. Similarly, anticipated events are more likely to have some sort of script in place before being actually experienced; hence unexpected events, like novel events, are better remembered.

The more the event breaks with your script for that type of event, the better your memory for that particular event will be. (Failures to remember trivial events, such as where you've put something, or whether you've done something, are reflections of the fact that we pay little attention to routine actions that are, as it were, already scripted.) To remember an event, you should select as many distinctive cues as possible. Some types of cue are more distinctive than others.

A Dutch psychologist called Willem Wagenaar kept a detailed diary for six years, recording for each event: *who* was involved, *what* the event was, *where* it occurred, and *when* it occurred. At the end of his study he was able to report that the best retrieval cue was *what*, followed by *who* and *where*, and lastly by *when*.

Most of the difference in the power of these details as cues derives from their relative distinctiveness: *what* is usually the most distinctive, while *when* is usually the least. The more routine the event of course, the less distinctive *what* is, and the greater the need to find something unusual to mark the event.

It's worth noting what a poor cue *when* is. Unfortunately, we are time-driven creatures, and we are often keen to know when something happened. Rather than remembering when, we usually have to work it out, by relating it to other events. It is therefore a good idea to have a number of landmark events readily accessible.

I have found dating events of the past ten years much easier because of the arrival of children in my life. Children are wonderfully useful for providing landmark events. Thus whenever I'm asked when we moved into our current house, I merely recall that we celebrated our son's third birthday in the new house soon after purchase, and from there (my son's current age being equally accessible!) I can work it out with ease.

The more landmark events – things that happen on dates that are memorable or important for you and so are readily accessible – you have the easier it is to relate a specific event to the nearest landmark. It is therefore worth your while to establish a number of landmark events at regular intervals. The more distinctive and memorable events in your life, the more landmark events you are likely to have.

Memory for other people

Personal memory also contains SOCIAL MEMORY, that memory for other people and their behaviour that enables you to form relationships and participate in a social group. Social memory contains the domain that is, more than any other domain, responsible for people's belief that their memory is a problem: IDENTITY MEMORY. Difficulty in remembering people's names is one of the most common memory tasks that people wish to be better at. And the reason for this is not that their memory is poor, but because it is so embarrassing when their memory lets them down.

We have, in fact, a remarkably good memory for other people's faces. Our memory domain for this particular type of information is not only capacious but also quite complex. Think about the ease with which you distinguish between hundreds, even thousands, of human faces, and then think about how hard it is to distinguish between the faces of birds, or dogs, or monkeys. This is not because human faces are any more distinctive than the faces of other animals. Think about how much harder it is for you to distinguish between the faces of people of an unfamiliar racial type, hence the old British saying: 'All Chinese look alike'.

Chinese faces are no less distinctive than European faces, but the differences between *any* human face are sufficiently subtle that they take a great deal of experience to learn. The importance of learning these subtle differences is shown in the way new babies focus on faces, and prefer them to other objects.

Our memory for other people is of course more than a memory for faces, although that part probably has the most impressive capacity. We also remember people's names and various biographical details. We can recognise people by hearing their voice, at a distance by seeing their shape or the way that they move, or even by their clothing. However, faces are the most common and reliable means of identifying a person.

There are three ways we can 'recognise' a person:

- We might recognise them as having been seen before, without recalling anything about them.
- We might identify them as a particular person, without recalling their name ('That's a friend of my son').
- We might identify them by name.

If you think about it you will realise that you never, ever, remember a person's name without knowing who she is. This is because names are held in a separate cluster to biographical details, and can only be accessed through the cluster holding those details. You also never recall information about a person without recognising them as familiar. While this sounds terribly obvious, there is actually a clinical condition whereby a person, while recognising the people around them, believes they have been replaced by doubles (impostors, robots, aliens, etc.). This is simply because the normal accompanying feeling of familiarity is missing.

There are three kinds of identity information that are important for recognising a person. Two of them are very obvious: the physical features, which are STRUCTURAL CODES, and the NAME CODE. The third is the SEMANTIC CODES, which are the biographical details, such as occupation, marital status and address. There is also a fourth type of code that is useful for remembering unfamiliar faces, VISUALLY DERIVED SEMANTIC CODES, such as age, gender and attributions like 'he looks honest/intelligent/sly'.

Semantic codes that are visually derived have an advantage over BIOGRAPHICAL CODES, because the link with the structural code is meaningful and thus strong, whereas the connection between the structural codes and biographical details is entirely arbitrary. To say someone looks like a fox connects meaningfully with the person's facial features, whereas to say that someone is a lawyer has no particular connection with the person's face (although to say someone *looks* like a lawyer would of course be meaningfully connected).

Visually derived semantic codes are useful for remembering new faces because the link with the physical features of the face is strong and meaningful. However you cannot *identify* a person without reference to the biographical codes.

The interesting aspect of these different codes is that you can only access them in a particular order: either from name to biographical details to physical features, or from physical features to biographical details to name. In other words, when you see someone, your mind doesn't directly go to the name, but passes first through the biographical information, such as their occupation. (This may happen so fast that you are not consciously aware of it, but you'll be conscious of it when the process is slower.) Similarly, when you think of someone's name, biographical details are called up before you recall the image of their face.

When you recognise a face as familiar but can't recall anything about the person, the structural code has failed to trigger the biographical code. When you identify a person by recalling details about them, but cannot recall their name, the biographical code has failed to trigger the name code.

From the list of 13 memory tasks that people most commonly are concerned about, four relate to identity memory:

- trying to put a name to a face
- trying to put a face to a name
- trying to remember who someone is (e.g. 'local librarian')
- meeting someone and wanting to remember details such as names of children and partner, any problems they may have been having last time you talked, etc.

We can now interpret these problems as follows:

PROBLEM	INTERPRETATION
trying to put a name to a face	accessing name code from structural code
trying to put a face to a name	accessing structural code from name code
trying to remember who someone is	accessing biographical code from structural code
trying to remember personal details	accessing event information from structural code

It's clear now why the third of these problems is the easiest: physical features and biographical details are directly linked. However, accessing a name code from the structural code (physical features) requires you first to access the biographical code. Whether the name code is then triggered depends on how strong the link between them is.

You will have noticed that in the last problem I suggested that event information was required, rather than the biographical code. Think of the common situation of seeing someone, knowing perfectly well who they are, but being at a loss to recall details that you know you need to mention, such as something you discussed last time you saw each other, or something you've heard about them.

Details such as what you may have talked about last time you met will be encoded in the event domain. Some details may even be encoded in the knowledge domain (for example, the films that a famous actor has appeared in). When you remember some details about a person but not others, it is likely that those details are encoded in a separate domain, and, because the link between them isn't strong enough, they haven't automatically activated with the biographical code.

In the main then, memory failures on these common identity tasks are due to weak links between the different codes. Therefore, to improve your memory for identity information, you should concentrate on strategies that strengthen the links between a) the structural codes and the biographical codes, and b) the biographical codes and the name code.

However, there is another weak point, and that is the structural codes themselves. As I have said, the differences between faces are subtle. Constructing an accessible structural code requires you to select features for encoding that will enable you to readily distinguish that particular face from others. Some faces, it must be said, make this very difficult.

In general, Caucasians tend to pay more attention to the upper half of the face – to the hair and eyes. Of course, this is not true of races whose hair and eyes tend to be much more similar. The mouth is also closely attended to, but, as with eyes, this is chiefly because the mouth and eyes are very informative as to a person's emotions. Although we attend to these features while in conversation with a person, we do not necessarily remember that information beyond that time. Interestingly the chin, then the cheeks, then lines, all seem to be attended to more than the nose (although the nose is often cited as a distinctive feature).

However, notwithstanding these generalisations, different people do focus on different facial features. I myself as a child categorised people by face shape. There is no rule that specifies which particular feature is more distinctive than another. What's important is what works for you.

Familiar faces tend to be encoded differently to new faces, and the difference suggests how we can more rapidly make a face familiar. Structural codes for familiar faces emphasise the more informative and less changeable features; for example, although initially we pay most attention to hair, hair is probably the most changeable feature we possess! The more familiar a person is, the less we are thrown by changes in hairstyle or hair colour. But we can completely fail to recognise someone we don't know well when they change their hair. To encode a new face effectively, focus on features that can't be changed.

Remembering how to do things

Skill memory belongs neither in knowledge memory nor any of the domains of personal memory, and is quite different from all the other kinds of information that have been discussed so far. It is often described as the distinction between knowing *how* and knowing *that*. It is generally agreed that practical knowledge must be organised quite differently to factual knowledge.

Acquisition of this type of information is thought to pass through three stages. The first stage is of course the instruction stage; a skill is first learned through verbal instruction. But this necessary first step is then succeeded by an ASSOCIATIVE STAGE, during which you coordinate the physical actions and strengthen the connections between successive actions. During this stage you still need verbal reminders to tell you what to do; however, in the third and final stage you lose the verbalisation entirely. Now, through practice of the action sequence you achieve autonomy; the skill becomes automatic, no thought is needed, and indeed thinking (verbalising) only serves to hinder your performance. A skill is not properly mastered until it becomes automatic.

For example, many of us have had the experience of trying to teach someone to drive a car. How often did you have to close your eyes and imagine yourself going through the motions before you could actually explain the sequence of movements needed? A skill is not truly acquired until, as we say, you can 'do it without thinking'. Having to think about what comes next only impedes the flow of actions.

Interestingly (and probably against common sense), there appears to be no mental limit to the AUTONOMOUS STAGE. Of course your physical condition sets a limit to how much improvement you can make to a practical skill (although, in practice, few people probably ever approach these limits), but a cognitive skill will continue to improve as long as you keep practising. One long-ago researcher had two people perform 10,000 mental addition problems, and they kept on increasing their speed to the end.

Practice makes perfect

Practice is crucial to mastering a skill. One of the critical aspects is assuredly the fact that, with practice, the demands on your attention get smaller and smaller.

While practice is the key, there are some actions we can take to ensure we get the most value out of our practice:

- Specific examples rather than abstract rules seem to be more important. Rules are eventually abstracted from examples, but examples continue to be important because they are more accessible.

- Feedback is very important. However to be beneficial it needs to occur while the action is active in memory. The next attempt also needs to occur while the feedback is active in memory.
- Skills learned under variable circumstances generalise better to new situations than skills learned under very rigid or specific circumstances. It's better to practise a skill with subtle variations (such as varying the force of your pitch, or the distance you are throwing) rather than trying to repeat your action exactly.
- Spacing your practice is probably even more important for skill learning than for learning factual information (maths text-books, for example, tend to put similar exercises together, but in fact they would be better spaced out).
- If skills share components with already mastered skills, learning will be easier (e.g. learning a tennis volley is easier if you have learnt a badminton volley).
- If a new skill contains steps that are contrary to steps contained in an already mastered skill, that new skill will be much harder to learn. (For example, when I changed my computer keyboard, the buttons for page up, page down, insert, etc. had been put in a different order. The conflict between the old habit and the new pattern made learning the new pattern harder than it would have been if I had never had a keyboard before.) The existing skill may also be badly affected.
- Whether or not it is better to try and learn a skill whole, or break it down into components and learn them separately, depends on whether the parts are independent (e.g. computer programming

can be broken into independent sub-skills, but learning to play the piano is best learned as a whole).

Remembering to do things

PLANNING MEMORY is sometimes termed future memory – a pleasantly paradoxical name. It contains your plans and goals (such as, 'I must pick up the dry-cleaning today'; 'I intend to finish this project within three months'). As with FORGETTING someone's name, forgetting to do something comes high on the list of memory tasks people would like to be better at, and for the same reason: forgetting to do something can often cause you much embarrassment.

Our intentions – the information in the planning domain – appear to be organised around goals. We remember goal-directed activities much more easily than other activities, and we remember the actual achievement of these goals best of all. But remembering intentions is much more difficult than remembering events that have happened, and the primary reason is the lack of retrieval cues. This is why, of all memory tasks, remembering to do things relies most heavily on memory aids outside our own minds. Reminder notes, calendars, diaries, watch-alarms, oven-timers, leaving objects in conspicuous places – all these external aids act as retrieval cues.

In general, when we form an intention, we link it either to an event ('After we go to the swimming-pool, we'll go to the supermarket') or a time ('At two o'clock I must ring Fred'). When, as so often, these TRIGGER EVENTS or times fail to remind us of our intention, it is because the link between the trigger and the intention is not strong enough. Partly this is because the trigger is not in itself particularly distinctive. Your failure to remember to ring Fred at two o'clock, for example, may be because you paid little attention to the clock reaching that time, or because there were other competing activities triggered by that same time signal.

Although planning memory has the disadvantage of poor and few retrieval cues, it does appear to compensate for this somewhat by being more easily triggered by quite marginal cues. Thus a friend of mine was reminded that her son's friend would be spending Saturday night with them when she saw an advertisement for a movie about John F. Kennedy (the child's father had the same initials: JFK).

Not all planning is linked to a trigger event or time. Quite a lot of planning simply waits upon an appropriate opportunity ('I must buy some stamps sometime'). Such intentions usually need quite explicit cues. Thus, if I happened to see stamps for sale, I would probably remember my intention, but walking past, or even into, a shop that happens to sell stamps, may not be enough to trigger my memory.

On the other hand, I might keep being reminded of my intention when I am in the same context as when I originally encoded the intention (when I am not in a position to carry it out!). Hence the increasing exasperation in not remembering a particular intention when you can do anything about it.

To deal with opportunistic planning, you should try to specify features of an appropriate opportunity when encoding the intention. Thus, to remember to buy bread on the way home, you should think about what actions you need to take to buy the bread (for example, going a different route) and try to form a strong link between the trigger event and your action. ('Today when I get to the traffic lights I'll turn *left*.')

A reminder of your intention is much less effective than being reminded of both the trigger event and the intended activity. Even being reminded of the trigger event is better than being reminded of the intention on its own. To remind yourself to do something, focus on the trigger, not the intent itself.

Don't assume that because something is important to you, you will automatically remember it; somewhat to their surprise, researchers have found no evidence that personal importance has any effect on the likelihood of remembering to do something.

Common memory problems and their domains

Having difficulty remembering facts (e.g. information you've studied, words, numbers or music)

→ knowledge memory.

Finding it hard to remember specific events (e.g. whether you've done something, where you've put something, when or where something happened, or important dates)

→ event memory.

Not being able to place people (e.g. put a name to a face, put a face to a name, who someone is, or someone's personal details)

→ identity memory.

Forgetting procedures (e.g. how to do something)

→ skill memory.

Forgetting to do something (e.g. to do something at a particular time, or can't think what you need to remember)

→ planning memory.

6 The memory you work with

So far we've been talking about memory as it's commonly thought of: as a database, the library of all our remembered thoughts and knowledge. Everything we've spoken of up to now – knowledge memory, autobiographical memory, skill memory, all the memory domains – are part of this database. But there is another type of memory, and that is the tiny fraction of your mind where you temporarily place those memories you're aware of at that moment. Obviously encoding occurs before the information is permanently stored. There must be a stage, a state of mind, in which the information is considered and selected. This is known as working memory.

Older books talk of working memory and the database as if they were different places. As if there were a table on which your papers are spread out (working memory) and a roomful of filing cabinets from which more files can be taken out (the database). It's a useful analogy of course, but the relationship between working memory and the database is more fluid than this. You don't have to clear some space on the table (working memory is a very small work space), trudge over to the cabinets, search for the next file you want, bring it back to the table, look at it, discover you need something else as well, make more room on the table (by picking up the papers and taking them with you to the cabinets and filing them), get the next file out of the cabinet . . . No, working memory and the database, the table and the filing cabinets, are not as separate as all that.

The idea today is not so much that working memory and the database are separately located memory stores, operating in different ways, but rather that they are different memory *processes* that create or *transform* memory codes. It is therefore somewhat misleading when we talk of information being 'in' working memory or 'in' the database. More accurately, we should say that information is in a working memory code (that is, an active code) or in a database code (a stored, passive code). This is not just a matter of academic pedantry.

Because working memory and the database are not completely separate entities, they can interact in a way which increases the capacity of working memory, and so increases the amount of information you can work on at one time. Instead of a small table and a room full of files, we have a theatre and a moving spotlight. The spotlight can grow or shrink, and be wide and diffuse or tightly focused.

In one regard, however, the analogy breaks down. Every time we relate our database to something in the outside world – an office, a library, a theatre – we have the same fundamental problem. In the world outside our mind, things have their place. A book and a lamp on a table beside a chair will stay a book and a lamp on a table beside a chair until and unless someone moves them. But the memories in your head dance.

The codes in the spotlight do not therefore have to be sitting together in the theatre. Imagine them instead in a ballroom. The codes waltz around the dance floor. Here two couples are dancing close together, there two couples change partners. The spotlight moves, its very action bringing about changes in the dancers. Quick! they say, hurrying over to get in the spotlight. In response to the dancers, the spotlight too changes. Oh, look at that arrangement! it thinks, and grows larger, more diffuse, to catch it all.

Some people have a better spotlight than others. It is more flexible, more responsive to the needs of the moment. It has a greater capacity to grow and illuminate more of the dancers at a time.

Your working memory capacity (how much information you can work with at one time) is a critical factor in determining your ability to take good notes, read efficiently, understand complex issues and reason. Indeed it may be that it is your working memory capacity that best 'measures' your intelligence.

Some people of course are born with a capacious flexible working memory. But it is not like eye colour, an attribute predetermined by your genes, and not subject to modification. You can increase your working memory capacity. But of course to do so, it helps to understand how working memory works, and how it interacts with the database.

Using your working memory

Essentially, working memory is the gatekeeper to the database. When you 'remember' something, you transform it from its database code into a working memory code – for, remember, you're only consciously aware of information in working memory. When you turn information into a memory code, you're transforming it from a working memory code into a permanent code in your database.

Let's consider that for a moment in terms of two common tasks.

Reading comprehension

Consider these two sentences:

> The spy quickly threw his report in the fire. The ashes floated up the chimney.

Perfectly comprehensible, yes? But the second sentence doesn't actually follow on directly from the first, unless you realise (as you assuredly did) that a) the report was on paper, and b) paper turns to ash in fire. Now I don't suppose you were aware of making those connections when reading those two sentences. We have a vast fund of knowledge that is so readily accessible that we don't have to think about it. Nevertheless, even though we are not aware of it, the knowledge still has to be accessed from memory.

Those two sentences were taken from an experimental study that looked at how people vary in their ability to fill in the missing connections. Clearly your ability to understand what you're reading or hearing depends to some extent on your skill at filling in the missing gaps. That skill probably depends on two main factors:

- how much information you can keep active at one time
- how quickly you can access the relevant information from your database.

Exercise 6.1

Read the following passages and answer the comprehension questions about them, without referring back to the text. (Text and questions taken from an experimental study by Daneman and Carpenter.)

> Sitting with Richie, Archie, Walter and the rest of the gang in the Grill yesterday, I began to feel uneasy. Robbie had put a dime in the juke box. It was blaring one of the latest 'Rock and Roll' favourites. I was studying, in horror, the reactions of my friends to the music. I was especially perturbed by the expression on my best friend's face. Wayne looked intense and

> was pounding the table furiously to the beat. Now, I like most of the things other teenage boys like. I like girls with soft blonde hair, girls with dark curly hair, in fact all girls. I like milkshakes, football games and beach parties. I like denim jeans, fancy T-shirts and sneakers. It is not that I dislike rock music but I think it is supposed to be fun and not taken too seriously. And here he was, 'all shook up' and serious over the crazy music.

Who was 'all shook up' and serious over the music?

> It was midnight and the jungle was very still. Suddenly the cry of a wolf pierced the air. This anguished note was followed by a flurry of activity. All the beasts of the jungle recognised that an urgent meeting had been summoned by the lion, their king. Representatives from each species made rapid preparations to get to the river clearing. This was where all such emergency assemblies were held. The elephant and tiger were the first to arrive. Next came the gorilla, panther and snake. They were followed by the owl and the crocodile. The proceedings were delayed because the leopard had not shown up yet. There was much speculation as to the reasons for the midnight alarm. Finally he arrived and the meeting could commence.

Who finally arrived?

In both passages, to understand the agent in the final sentence you must remember the reference in an earlier sentence. In the latter passage, this reference is only two sentences earlier, but in the first passage, the reference is six sentences back. Readers with a low capacity for information of this type have difficulty with a reference more than two or three sentences back.

Mental arithmetic

Doing sums in your head requires you to have a store of well-learned sums and products ($6 + 7 = 13$, $3 \times 3 = 9$ and so on). These might be considered the alphabet of arithmetic calculation. When attempting to calculate, say, $45 + 32$, you will use the known sums of $4 + 3$ and $5 + 2$. But you also need to remember the first 7 while you retrieve the second 7, and that's where working memory is needed.

Many errors in mental arithmetic occur because the person has failed to hold all the partial solutions in working memory. Remembering one 7 while you retrieve a second 7 doesn't seem very hard, but what about a problem like $4735 + 629$? You have to hold in working memory not only each retrieved sum ($5 + 9$, $3 + 2$, $7 + 6$) but also the carried amounts. And of course, you must remember not only the values of the sums, but also their order.

Your working memory capacity is critical in determining your skill at understanding, thinking and calculating.

Differences between working memory and the database

Probably the most important difference between active working memory codes and passive database codes is the way in which the codes are maintained. A memory code in its passive stored state is maintained effortlessly. It may be destroyed by physical damage; it may become corrupted by later amendments; it may become hard to find by not being retrieved for many years. But it is maintained without your conscious attention. The capacity of your database, your success in finding particular memory codes, their resistance to corruption or damage, all these depend, as we have seen, on one major factor: organisation.

However, an active working memory code is a temporary state which cannot be maintained for more than a few seconds without your conscious attention. It is this which so limits working memory capacity.

There is also an important difference in the nature of the memory codes: while information in the database tends to be recorded in terms of its meaning (a SEMANTIC CODE), information in working memory tends to be encoded in terms of its sound (an ACOUSTIC code). This explains why the most common method of maintaining information in working memory is to repeat it aloud.

Improving your working memory codes

I said that people vary in their working memory capacity, and this is true. I also said that it is possible to increase that capacity, and this is true in one sense. Researchers have had very limited success in changing what might be thought of as 'fixed' capacity – the number of chunks you can hold at one time. Where training and effort can really help is in this interaction between working memory and the database, in the ability to organise large amounts of information into one chunk.

Repetition

Information is held in working memory through rehearsal, that is, by repeating the information over and over again to ourselves. Most of us use this strategy when we are given a phone number and we just want to hold it in our minds long enough to write it down, or ring the number. We are all familiar with the ease with which this information is lost as soon as something or someone interrupts us. The name for this process is MAINTENANCE REHEARSAL (*rehearsal* to *maintain* information in working memory). Mostly, repeating to oneself in this way is only sufficient to hold the information for as long as you are rehearsing it. As soon as you stop, the information is gone.

Simple repetition, therefore, while it can help you *recognise* information (a face, a fact, a word), is not much use in helping *recall*. This is because it maintains items in a speech (acoustic) code and doesn't form links with potential semantic retrieval cues. It can however, assist recall when acoustic information is a distinctive part of the memory code, as long as you are using acoustic cues in your generation strategy.

It is the need for your attention that limits the capacity of working memory. You can only hold as much as you can attend to at one time. It's like juggling: as long as you keep the balls moving you're fine, but once the number of balls increases to the point where you lose track of one or more balls, you're sunk. The balls come tumbling down. The information is lost. Some people are better jugglers than others. But like most things, it's a matter of practice, not simply native ability.

There are of course defined physical limits on the number of balls it is possible to juggle, no matter how much practice you have. Expert jugglers don't amaze by juggling 30 balls; they amaze by changing the nature of what they juggle. Juggling five fiery torches is more impressive than juggling five balls. Similarly, although you can slightly increase your working memory capacity by increasing your ability to attend to a number of different things at once, you will have a much greater effect by changing the nature of your information chunks.

Chunking

Chunk, although it doesn't sound like it, is the technical term for the bits of information that working memory deals with. Chunks are the juggling balls in the example above. It is any unit of information organised according to some rule or pattern.

Probably the most widely known fact about working memory is that it can only hold around seven chunks of information (between five and nine). However, this tells us little about the limits of working memory because the size of a chunk is indeterminate.

For example, if you have to remember a phone number, each digit might represent a chunk. Say the number is 478 6923. If you treat each digit as a separate piece of information, as when you simply repeat it, remembering the phone number (seven digits) takes up all your working memory capacity, and you have no attention to spare for anything else until you have finished with the number. (Note also that you should always pause in the same places whenever you repeat the sequence: if you said 4, 78, 69, 23, the first time, and then 478, 692, 3, the next time, and then 47, 86, 92, 3, you would be trying to learn three different sequences.)

However, if you want to remember the number for a long time, then you might try to find something about the relationship between the digits to make it easier to remember. For example, you could divide it into three chunks: 478, 69, 23. Or two: 478, 6923. If you related all the digits to each other, the seven-digit phone number would become one chunk.

A chunk may be thought of as a pronounceable label; it is, after all, a type of cluster, and the extent to which it can be treated as an integrated unit is determined by whether it can be given a single label.

Chunking increases the amount of information you can hold in working memory. What governs the size of a chunk is meaning, and meaning is quite personal: what has meaning for me will not necessarily have any meaning for you.

Chunking and meaning

People can usually repeat back four nonsense syllables, such as:
sul kol fek gix
but not six:
ryn deq cuz gyt pob ved.
They can repeat back six one-syllable words:
cat dog ram hit law fig
but not nine one-syllable words:
log hat dim run tin pot wax sun lip.
They can repeat back three four-syllable words (equalling 12 syllables):
dictionary illustrious responsible coronation
but not six four-syllable words:
chameleon dromedary duplication mechanism evolution statistical.
But they can repeat back a 19-word sentence!
Material that has been well learned will be more strongly encoded, and thus it can be more quickly activated.

I have discussed this as if it is critically the *number* of chunks that determines whether your work space is full. However, some recent research has suggested that the limiting factor is actually the time it takes you to say the words. It appears that you can only hold in working memory what you can say in 1.5–2 seconds. Slow speakers are therefore penalised.

The importance of verbal rehearsal is of course because working memory codes are usually sound-based. Of course not all information can be expressed in an acoustic code. Some, for example, may be expressed in images. There may indeed be a number of different working spaces: one for material that is heard, one for material that is seen, one for material that is smelt, one for material that is felt, etc. At this stage, little is known about the way information from senses other than ears and eyes is processed.

Exercise 6.2

Find some way of meaningfully relating the digits in these three different chunking patterns:

1. 478, 69, 23
2. 478, 6923
3. 4786923

Measuring your working memory capacity

Because there are several different components within working memory, there is no single measure of working memory capacity. Your capacity for numbers may well be quite different from your capacity for words, and different again from your capacity for visual images.

Digit span

This refers to the number of digits that you can correctly repeat back, in the correct order. A normal, unpractised person has a DIGIT SPAN of between four and eleven digits. You can increase your span slightly by practising the skill. You can increase it markedly by developing effective encoding strategies (and practising them). Basically it comes down to chunking: you need to practise seeing groups of digits as meaningful chunks.

To do this successfully you need some well-learned structure.

Some people, for example, have used sports statistics, or addresses and dates. Others have found transforming digits into pounds and pence makes them more meaningful. Others find mathematical relationships memorable (e.g. 632 is memorable if you transform it into $6 \div 3 = 2$).

Word span

How many words you can hold in working memory depends on a) how long the words are, and b) how much they sound the same (you can maintain more dissimilar words). Your WORD SPAN affects your ability to repeat back unfamiliar words, and therefore is critical to vocabulary acquisition. Your child's quickness in mastering language, and your own ability to 'pick up' a foreign language, are both partly determined by this aspect of your working memory.

Reading span

Your ability to repeat back unfamiliar words is critical to your learning of new words, but your ability to understand complex sentences (your READING SPAN) appears to be governed by a separate aspect of working memory.

To measure your own digit, word and reading spans, see the Quick reference section on page 163.

Expanding your working memory capacity

Working memory capacity is not only about storage – about how *much* information you can hold at one time. After all, it's called *working* memory for a reason: because it contains the information you are working with. The processing of information also takes some of your resources. The more resources the processing needs, the less capacity you have available for storage, therefore the less information you can hold. The more skilled you are at processing, the more room you have for information.

In other words, whatever your working memory capacity, you can increase it by practising appropriate strategies to such a level of mastery that your processing requirements are minimal (the more practised you are, the less the processing demands).

A larger working memory capacity helps you:

- make better chunks
- build more links
- abstract themes
- integrate new codes with old.

A larger working memory capacity therefore gives you a head-start, but the rules are still the same. The important thing is not whether your working memory capacity is high or low, but whether you have mastered appropriate strategies for encoding information. Knowing your capacity is useful however, in helping you decide what strategies are most useful to you.

Part two

Strategies

7 Using your memory

Do you remember, right at the beginning of this book, I talked about how we shouldn't say, 'I want to improve my memory', but rather, 'I want to improve these specific memory skills'? Now that you understand that there are a number of different memory domains, all organised in different ways, I hope you can see exactly why you need to use various strategies to improve your memory for different things.

Clearly, if you want to improve your ability to remember names, this is going to require a specific strategy that focuses on that connection between the name code and the memory codes for the physical features of the face. But if it's your memory for intended actions that's your concern, you'll know now to pay particular attention to the trigger event, and focus on strategies that emphasise the connection between that and the intention. If you want to improve your ability to learn new skills (say, computer skills), you'll realise the necessity of lots of practice, and concentrate on strategies for getting the most out of your practice.

Now that you understand the broad principles of how memory works, we can take the next step: improving specific memory tasks.

Why do you want to improve your memory?

Now that we've reached the point of looking at specific skills to aid memory, you need to ask yourself *why* you want to improve your memory. Why, specifically, do you think you have a 'poor' memory?

Here are the memory tasks that most commonly cause problems:

- trying to put a name to a face
- trying to put a face to a name
- trying to remember who someone is (e.g. 'local librarian')
- remembering important dates (birthdays, appointments, etc.)
- remembering to do something at a particular time
- remembering information you have studied
- remembering the names of things (e.g. computer jargon, business strategies, books, plants, recipes, etc.)
- trying to remember how to do something (e.g. computer procedures, craft techniques, domestic tasks)
- meeting someone and wanting to remember details such as names of children and partner, any problems they may have been having last time you talked, etc.
- knowing there's something you need to remember but you can't think what it is
- remembering whether you've done something
- remembering where you've put something
- remembering when/where something happened (e.g. where you bought something, where you read something).

Be specific. Think of particular occasions when you have been embarrassed by your memory failure, or annoyed with yourself over your forgetfulness. Write them down. Use these specific instances as a springboard for working out your needs. If you were mortified the time you forgot your best friend's birthday, write that down. Then consider whether this points to a general memory task you want to be better at (remembering significant dates), or whether you merely want to ensure a better memory for one or two dates of particular importance.

If specific instances of memory failure point to general memory tasks that you wish to be better at, write down the general task. If only the specific instance is of interest to you, write down the specific task.

Here is an example:

> Memory tasks I want to be better at:
>
> remembering personal details that my friends tell me
>
> remembering interesting things I read
>
> remembering the names of people at my tennis club
>
> remembering my partner's and my nieces' birthdays
>
> remembering things I have to do today
>
> remembering information I have studied.

If you want to achieve genuine memory improvement, this is a vital, utterly necessary step. So do take the time to think about what you want to achieve before going any further.

The cost of memory skills

Another thing to consider when assessing your memory needs and the strategies you might use – a factor too little considered by most memory training programmes – is the costs of particular learning strategies.

For example, one of the classic memory strategies is the 'method of loci' (see page 126). This strategy requires you to memorise some physical object that has distinct locations (for example, your house, a familiar route, a classroom). You then use this structure as a base for any information you want to remember. So for a shopping list, you might picture bread on the doormat, potatoes hanging from the coat-hook, apples in the sink, and so on. This strategy was supposedly invented in 477 BC, and people have been learning it ever since – but how many people have ever used it more than once or twice? It involves more effort than most of us want to put in.

Strategies such as the method of loci and the pegword system (see page 127) do work, but very few people want to put in the effort to making them work. That's not laziness, but an appreciation of costs versus benefits. The cost of using these strategies is rarely worth the benefits. The cost of having an old envelope stuck to the fridge with a magnet, and writing down shopping needs as they come up, is much less than the mental effort needed for me to produce vivid mental images for each item I need.

For a strategy to have value it must be not only effective but also useful. That means the benefit of it *to you* must be worth the cost *to you*. Some people find it very easy to create memorable images, and for them the cost of such a strategy is low. Some people may rate a particular memory task as so important to them that they are prepared to invest a great deal of time and effort into improving skills that would help them. Before you learn a skill, assess whether it is worth the time and effort to you.

Look at your list of the memory tasks you are poor at. Now ask yourself: how important are these tasks to you? You may be very poor at remembering people's names, but perhaps you don't really care. You may already be reasonably competent at remembering information you have studied, but perhaps it is really important to you to be better.

Beside the tasks on your list, put a rating as to how much effort you're prepared to put into improving your skills for that task. The ratings could be simple comments indicating the amount of effort you're prepared to put in ('lots', 'not much', 'some', etc.), or could be numbers indicating your priority order. You may find doing both helpful. Here's an example of what your table would look like, using some common memory complaints:

MEMORY TASK	EFFORT RATING	PRIORITY RATING
remembering information you have studied		
remembering someone's name/face		
remembering important dates		
remembering to do something		

Now that you have your targets worked out, let's see what you need to do to achieve them.

Be confident

Confidence in a particular technique doesn't come about merely because you have been told it's really useful, nor even by trying it out yourself. To be really convinced of a strategy's usefulness, you need to experience for yourself its use in everyday situations, and you need to understand *why* it works. You also need to believe in your own ability to use the strategy successfully and appropriately – to do that you need to *master* the skill, not simply 'learn' it.

Think of driving a car. In the beginning there were so many different things to think about, but eventually they became routine, automatic. As it is with driving a car, playing the piano and pruning the roses, a memory skill is mastered when it becomes automatic. And once it becomes automatic, you're safe! An automatic, over-learned skill is part of your 'permastore'. Like the permafrost that never melts, memories in permastore are never lost.

More importantly, if the skill can be performed automatically, the cost of applying it falls dramatically. The time is less; the effort is much less. Reducing the cost makes using the skill a much more attractive proposition. An over-learned skill is therefore much more likely to be used.

Mastering a memory skill means making it a habit. You are more likely to use a skill if:

- you are convinced it helps you remember
- you understand why it helps you remember
- you know when and when not to use it
- you are confident that you can use the skill.

I believe part of the reason for people's lack of confidence in their own skills is the association we commonly make between learning and intelligence. If a person appears to learn facts easily, we assume they are intelligent. A person who has trouble learning is assumed to be less intelligent. Although of course some people find it easier than others to learn appropriate skills and see when to apply them effectively, being skilled at learning is a learned skill. You can be 'clever' and poor at learning; you can be 'average' and good at learning. Whether or not you *use* memory-improvement strategies depends more on how much you know about your memory processes than how intelligent you are.

The key to good learning lies not only in your knowledge of how memory works, and your flexible and appropriate use of different strategies, but also in your ability to understand your own capabilities. You're not likely to use efficient strategies if you don't even realise how poorly you have learned something or how unlikely you are to remember it. You are not going to apply a strategy well if you are blithely unaware that you have completely misunderstood the information.

An effective learner:

- knows how memory works
- has many memory skills and can apply them appropriately
- monitors and understands their own learning behaviour.

I hope that you have now, after going through the first part of this book, a good understanding of the basic process of memory. In the next chapter we are going to look a little more deeply into the different sorts of memory task there are, and learn which tasks demand different types of strategies. Subsequent chapters will explore these different learning and memory strategies. But gaining this knowledge will only take you so far: to gain confidence in your abilities, you need to practise! The exercises provided will start you off with that, so do make sure you do them.

8 Strategies to improve your learning

I said at the beginning of this book that memory is not a single thing, and I hope you can now see how true that is. With different memory processes going on for your knowledge of facts and words, your knowledge of people, of the events and experiences that make up your life, of the physical and mental skills you can do, and of the tasks you plan to do, it's clear that the strategies you need for dealing with one type of information won't do for another. One strategy, however good, isn't going to cut it. You need a whole toolbox. Most importantly, you need to know which tool to use.

Our aim, then, is to match memory strategies with the appropriate memory tasks. But there are a great many memory strategies, ranging from the very specific (*E*very *G*ood *B*oy *D*eserves *F*ruit, for learning the notes on the lines of the treble clef) to the very general (MONITORING your learning). To help us in our task of matching the right strategy to the specific task, it helps to be able to reduce the number of strategies we need to consider. We need a classification system.

In general, we can divide memory strategies into two broad categories: information manipulation strategies, and SUPPORT STRATEGIES. The more specific strategies are those that manipulate the information you wish to remember (such as the *E*very *G*ood *B*oy *D*eserves *F*ruit mnemonic), while support strategies are more general strategies that help you learn more effectively (such as monitoring your learning).

Information manipulation strategies can be further subdivided between strategies for information that needs to be memorised verbatim and those for information that needs to be understood and remembered for meaning. As discussed in the first part, rote memorisation and 'true' learning are quite different goals that require very different strategies. In this chapter we will look at information-manipulation strategies for meaningful information.

Understand, select and attend

I will use the term STUDY STRATEGIES as a convenient shorthand for encoding strategies that are aimed at helping your understanding and recall of meaningful information.

To encode meaningful information for better recall we must understand it, and we must understand it sufficiently well that we can select the information that needs to be given special attention. USA – Understand, Select, Attend – these are the processes underlying our study strategies. The effective use of any study strategy hinges on your ability to select and attend to the important information. Your evaluation of any specific strategy is based on this fundamental principle.

Study strategies are valuable to the extent that they help you understand the information and distinguish the important information from the less important. The two main study strategies are ACTIVE READING and TAKING NOTES. Both of these are general strategies containing a number of more specific strategies.

Active reading

Reading is in itself quite a passive process. Successful students tend to read actively, that is, they think about the information they are reading, ask themselves questions about it, and try to relate it to information they already have. Poor students on the other hand, tend to simply read, and their primary strategy to help their understanding and memory of the material is simply to re-read it. There are a number of active reading strategies.

One well-known, but frequently misunderstood active reading strategy is SKIMMING. Many people believe this is a poor strategy, which is hardly surprising when you realise that skimming has been variously described as: reading only the first and last words of a sentence; reading very fast; missing out the long words. In fact, if done well, skimming is a very effective strategy, for it is all about actively searching text for critical information.

Reading is a complex skill that takes place at a number of levels. In the first place, the physical features of the letters must be recognised and interpreted, then the words, the meaningful chunks of phrases, and the idea stated in a sentence. Many readers go no further than this, but an effective reader goes beyond, to the level of main ideas and of themes. But a reader who attends only to the 'higher' levels – to the main ideas and themes – risks missing significant details. Attention must be paid to each level of the decoding process. For most of us, the first levels – the decoding of letters and words – is such a practised skill that we need expend little resources on them. Decoding at higher levels may require considerably more attention. Bearing in mind the limited capacity of working memory, you should accordingly focus on only one level at one time. Thus, if the material is particularly complex, you would attack it first chunk by chunk, then at the sentence-level (ideas), then at paragraph-level (main ideas), before trying to grasp the theme at section-level.

Active reading strategies include the following:

Search strategies:

- jumping forward or backward in the text to find particular information
- skimming through the text for particular information
- anticipating information that might be covered in the text, and hunting for it

Clarifying strategies:

- backtracking for clarification
- attending to figures and tables
- re-stating text in own words

Elaborating strategies:

- moving back and forth between different parts (perhaps between a table and the text) to integrate them
- thinking of analogies or examples
- drawing conclusions

Evaluating strategies:

- evaluating the difficulty of the text, and how well you are understanding it
- noting whether information is previously known

- evaluating the relevance of the information to your own goals
- evaluating the quality of the information.

Active reading is about understanding. The crucial test in deciding how useful an active reading strategy is to you is whether it helps you understand the information.

Taking notes

The sort of information for which we use a note-taking strategy (information from books; information from a formal spoken presentation) comes to us already packaged. Someone has produced the material, and the same specific note-taking strategies have probably been used, to a greater or lesser extent, to help you understand and remember the information. Each of these strategies therefore has two aspects: as a *strategy* that you can use to render information more comprehensible and memorable, and as a *cue* to the level of difficulty of the material and its organisation.

Most people probably believe that they are taking notes to provide a written record of information they need to remember. But research reveals that the primary value of note-taking is through its effect on how you encode the information. For this reason, note-taking is effective to the extent that you paraphrase, organise and make sense of the information while taking notes. Notes that are simply taken down verbatim, without thought, are not likely to be effective (unless of course you later rewrite and reorganise them).

Studying for an exam

You should study the material to be examined at the same time of day that the exam is scheduled for. The longer the delay between your studying and the exam, the more separated you should make the gaps between your periods of study. This helps increase the chance that at least one of the study contexts will match the exam context (in terms of the weather, your mood, your state of mind, and so on).

The longer the expected time until the test, the more advantageous a long time between study periods will be. The longer the test delay, the less study and test contexts are likely to overlap, therefore the more important it is that the two study contexts should vary as much as possible.

If the time of the test is known, massed study just before the test is better – study and test contexts (at least as regards mood and mental attitude) are more likely to be similar.

Cramming just before an exam is no good for remembering in the long-term, however – again, partly because of context. By maximising the similarity between the learning and the recall contexts, you have improved your chance of remembering the information in that particular context, but you don't have the experience of encoding the material in a number of different contexts that you need to assist recall in different situations.

Several factors affect whether or not note-taking is effective:

- how fast the information is presented (note-taking is more likely to aid recall if presentation rate is slow and you can review your notes)

- the density/complexity of the information
- the style of the presentation (for example, a very formal, 'dry' text is more likely to be recorded verbatim while a more informal passage is more likely to be paraphrased)
- how well the information is organised
- how skilled you are at taking notes (in particular, your skill at capturing the most important points).

From these we can generate several useful rules for effective note-taking:

- Select: omit trivial and redundant details. Omit anything you'll recall anyway!
- Condense: replace lists with a category term.
- Organise: choose HEADINGS and topic sentences.
- Rephrase: use your own words.

Note in particular the instruction to omit anything you'll remember anyway. This is trickier than it might sound. We feel that, of course, we must note down the most important facts, but often the most important facts are the ones we'll remember anyway. The information we really need to record is the middle-tier information – the information that is not *the* most important, but is important nonetheless. Note-taking is usually performed in a situation where time is limited. Time taken to record information that you will remember without noting it, is time taken from noting down less memorable information.

Note-taking is a strategy for making information meaningful. With this in mind, let's look at the component strategies of note-taking.

Highlighting

HIGHLIGHTING refers to any means of emphasising key words or phrases, such as underlining, framing, using bold type, using a coloured marker, etc. As a cue, it is effective in helping you remember highlighted details, but at the expense of other information. While it does cue you to the details the author regarded as important, how useful that is to you depends on how well the author's goals match your own.

As a strategy, highlighting is useful as a means of focusing your attention, and it encourages you to spend more time on the material. For both these reasons, therefore, it improves your recall of both the highlighted details *and* the rest of the text.

But highlighting is only effective in certain conditions. Because part of its value lies in encouraging you to spend more time, it's only useful when you have sufficient time. Because its value is in focusing your attention on key concepts, it's only effective with material that isn't too dense (doesn't have too many important ideas), and material that isn't too difficult (ideas too complex to convey by key words or phrases). For the same reason, the material needs to require only one or two different types of cue, and it's best if you can restrict yourself to only one highlighted phrase per paragraph. And of course, how effective your highlighting is depends wholly on your skill in selecting key concepts!

Headings

A story has a very clear and strong shape that we all incorporate from a young age. In stories, the narrative is held together by a CAUSAL CHAIN – a string of causal connections from the protagonist's goal to the outcome. To the extent that this chain is clear, the story will be easy to remember.

Explanatory text, however, tends to be more disconnected than the average story (and hence more difficult to remember, for your recall depends heavily on how well connected the information is). Accordingly a number of strategies have been devised for emphasising changes of topic and the organisational structure of the text. One such strategy is the use of headings.

As a cue then, headings are valuable to the extent that they link changes of topic. Unsurprisingly therefore, headings are little needed if the text has few changes of topic. Headings can also act as labels for clusters. When you use them that way, of course, you need to later use those same labels as retrieval cues. For both these reasons – as connectives between and labellers of topics – headings can help you produce better summaries.

As a strategy, you can apply your own headings as you restructure the text. This is a useful strategy when the text is not organised in this fashion, or it's poorly done, or when the author's goals and interests are not the same as yours. Creating your own headings can help you abstract section themes, by forcing you to concisely encapsulate the main point.

To assess whether the headings provided in a text are of value to you, ask yourself whether they highlight the main points and themes, provide meaningful connections between topics and provide good retrieval cues.

Exercise 8.1

Go through chapter seven and note down the headings and subheadings. Now look at each section and write down what you think is its main point under each section heading. Do the headings bear on the main points? Are the headings short enough, or do they contain a key word or phrase that would be a useful retrieval cue? Can you think of better ones?

Summaries

Summaries recap the main points without adding any new information or offering a new perspective. They may be a straightforward string of factual statements (TOPICAL SUMMARIES) or they may reorganise text into a different format (GRAPHIC SUMMARIES); for example, in the form of OUTLINES, GRAPHIC ORGANISERS, MULTIMEDIA SUMMARIES or MAPS.

Here is an example of what is considered a 'normal' summary – a topical summary. This is a brief summary of part of chapter three:

> Memory codes are easily accessed when they have strong links.
>
> Links are strengthened by being used frequently.
>
> Some activation remains in an activated link for a time, making it easier to reactivate.
>
> To encode new information so that it will be accessible, you need to connect it meaningfully with existing strong codes.
>
> Repeating information strengthens its code, but repeating it at spaced intervals, in different contexts, increases the number and strength of its links.
>
> The links between codes make them meaningful, but meaning is greater when a single theme integrates linked codes.
>
> To ensure linked codes are integrated by a single theme, and to provide a retrieval cue, clusters should have an identifying label.

> The more strong links there are between codes in a cluster, the more likely it is to be treated as a single unit, facilitating recall of all the information contained in it.
>
> The more links between codes, the more potential recall cues.

To summarise effectively it is critical that you restate the main ideas and themes in your own words. It is a poor strategy to copy out the sentences that look important and ignore the rest. If there was no value in those intervening sentences, the author wouldn't have bothered writing them! A good summary sentence condenses the important information in a paragraph into a new statement. It is a good idea therefore to try and produce summaries without looking at the text. The extent to which summarising is an effective strategy depends on your skill at distinguishing important information from less important.

Outlines and graphic organisers are useful strategies for hierarchical information. Compare the following two examples (taken from Robinson and Kiewra, 1995). The first is an outline and the second is a graphic organiser.

Schizophrenia

I.	Simple		
	A.	% of Americans	1/10
	B.	Symptoms:	Gradual withdrawal and disinterest in the world
	C.	Severity:	Most likely to fend for themselves
II.	Paranoid	% of Americans	1
		Symptoms:	Feeling of being persecuted
		Severity:	May live in a marginal way

III.	Catatonic	% of Americans	1/10
		Symptoms:	Peculiar motor behaviour alternating between stupor and frenzy
		Severity:	Series of short attacks over many years
IV.	Hebephrenic	% of Americans	3/4
		Symptoms:	Regressive behaviour and total disregard for personal hygiene
		Severity:	Most severe

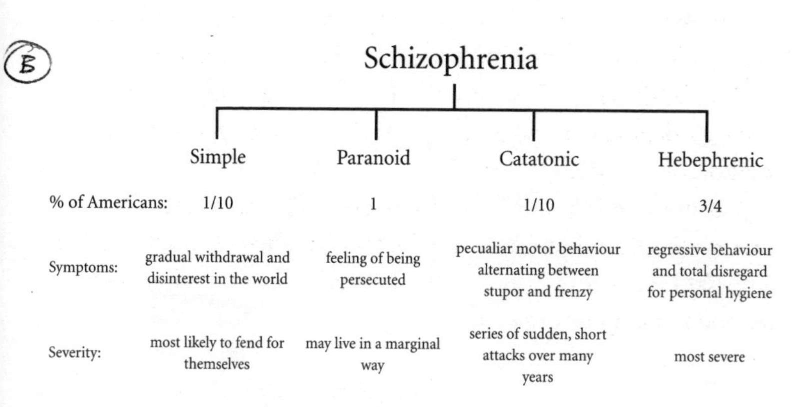

Outlines are easier to produce than graphic organisers – hence their popularity – but in general they are less effective. In the outline, the clusters *within* a concept are clear, but the relations *between* concepts – between the clusters – are not. A graphic organiser allows connections between clusters to be more readily seen.

Multimedia summaries are particularly appropriate (and valuable) for scientific explanations. In multimedia summaries pictures and words are combined, as below.

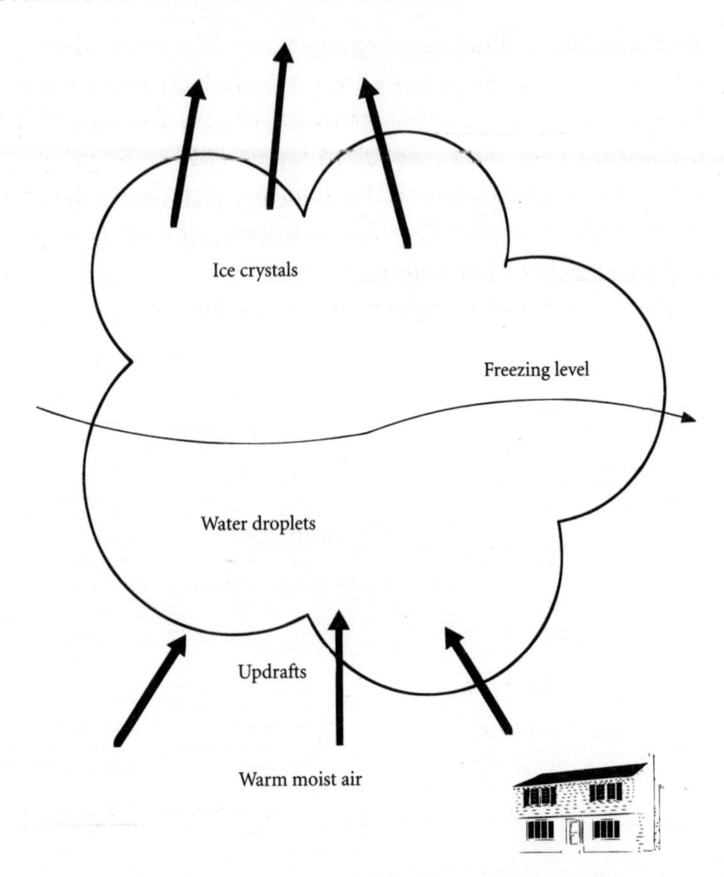

1. Warm moist air rises, water vapour condenses and forms clouds

This is the first picture in a description of how lightning occurs (taken from Mayer et al.).

To create an effective multimedia-summary, you need to be very concise, and use a minimum of text. Most crucially (and this is where many such summaries fall down), words and images need to be coordinated. A multimedia-summary that doesn't put the relevant text close to the image it belongs to will not be effective.

Probably the most widely-useful type of summary is a map.

Although several different mapping strategies have been developed (MIND-MAPPING is of course well known), the basic idea is the same for them all: information is organised into a 'map' that graphically displays the main points and clusters them into useful groupings. The essential characteristic is that information is *not* displayed in a linear or hierarchical fashion. A map begins in the centre of a page, and works out in all directions.

Here is a partially-completed map of chapter six:

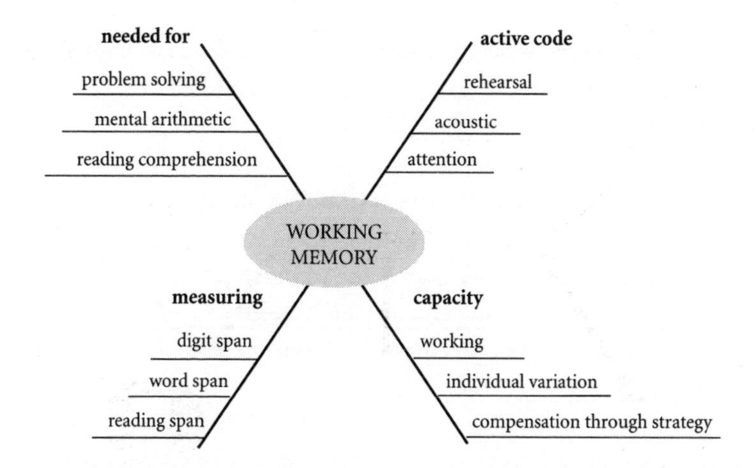

The essence of a map is that it provides a retrieval structure. Producing the map helps to organise the information, and once produced, provides a summary for later review. The map also emphasises new vocabulary – a large part of science learning concerns the learning of technical terms.

A crucial step in the strategy is the attempt to recall details without looking at the text. By making yourself dredge for the information, you will be forcing yourself to dig out related information from your existing store of knowledge.

When constructing a map of this kind, the first thing to do is select a key word. Write it in the centre of your page and draw several lines extending out from it. Now skim the text to select secondary headings, and write these headings on the lines radiating from the key word. For the next step it's important that you don't consult the text; instead, recall as many details as you can without looking at the text and add them to the map. Now you can re-read the text and add any important details that you've missed.

Exercise 8.2

See how many more details you can add to the map of chapter five without referring to the text, then check back and add more.

Building on the given information

A key component of any search for understanding requires that you link the information being presented with related information that you have in your database. Such connections are achieved through elaboration.

Elaborative strategies were developed in the context of learning pairs of associated items, such as when you learn that *aronga* mean 'direction' in Maori. The elaboration in this context could involve joining the two items into a common phrase or image (e.g. 'You're going in the *wrong direction*'), thus forming a link between them.

While language learning (foreign languages; new vocabulary in your native language; technical jargon) is all about linking pairs of words, such learning is of little direct practical relevance to most classes of information that we want to remember. But the basic concept of elaboration is easily extended to more complex material.

Consider the following text, imagining that you wish to learn the biographical facts about this (fictitious) person (the example is taken from a 1987 study by McCormick and Levin):

> Born and raised on a dairy *farm* where she helped take care of the cows, *Charlene McKune* has always been used to hard work. When she was a child, McKune enjoyed creating homes for her pets out of her toy *building blocks*. To earn extra money and because of her hatred for dirt of any kind, McKune began *washing cars* for her parents' friends.

The italicised words highlight the critical information.

One method of elaborating this information to make it more memorable would be to transform it into an interactive image (TRANSFORMATIONAL ELABORATION – this strategy is discussed in the next chapter). By coding the proper name (*Charlene McKune*) as an imageable similar-sounding word (*raccoon*), the highlighted information can be transformed into a mental picture of a pet *raccoon* outside a *farm*house jumping over a long row of *building blocks* with some children *washing cars* nearby.

A second strategy (NON-TRANSFORMATIONAL ELABORATION) involves abstracting a unifying theme and rewriting the information as an integrated cluster around this theme:

> *Charlene McKune* spent much of her life living in the serenty of the remote countryside. Born and raised on a *farm*, McKune grew to love the peace and quiet of rural living. When she was a child, her father made her *building blocks* out of bits of wood on the farm, and McKune spent hours building 'barns' and 'silos' with these blocks. To earn extra money, McKune began *washing cars* – and sometimes tractors – for the neighbouring farmers.

There are pros and cons to each of these ways of building on the given information. Transformational strategies introduce relationships into the to-be-learned material, connecting ideas that are not always naturally linked. While they can aid memory, because the relationships are arbitrary, they don't help you understand the material. Non-transformational strategies, on the other hand, build on the meaningful and natural connections that are already present, and aid understanding, as well as memory. These strategies are crucial for developing true expertise and mastery of a subject, but because they require you to dig deep into the meaning of the material, exploring the connections it has with other information you know, you may have to work harder at applying them.

Exercise 8.3

Can you abstract the unifying theme of the second passage about Charlene McKune?

If the critical information to learn had been *cows*, *hard work*, *pets*, *hating dirt*, what might the theme be? Can you rewrite the passage to reflect this theme?

Ask 'why?'

One way of building on the information given to you is turning the facts into why-questions. This is a non-transformational strategy known as ELABORATIVE INTERROGATION. The idea behind the strategy is that relevant prior knowledge is not always readily activated when you are trying to learn new information, and sometimes help is needed to make the right connections. The strategy requires you to go beyond the information given to you and to construct reasons for the relationships between bits of information.

For example, consider the following passage (taken from a 1990 study by Woloshyn, Willoughby, Wood and Pressley):

> The park-like atmosphere at the University of Calgary is partially maintained by the school's policy that no cars be allowed on campus. Some of Canada's best research institutes, like the Arctic Institute of North America, are located on or near the campus. The university also has a wilderness information and communication center on campus. The school has a theatre that is modelled on Stratford. The school's art museum has a very fine collection of ancient coins. Unfortunately, the school offers very few intramural sports.

The elaborative interrogation strategy involves turning the facts to be learned into why-questions and then answering them. Essentially the questions ask why a particular fact should be true. For example: Why does the University of Calgary campus have a park-like atmosphere? Why are some of the country's best research institutes located on or near this campus? Why does the university have a wilderness information and communication centre on campus?

The effectiveness of this strategy does not require you to know the correct answers to these questions; the important thing is that you think about them (though it does help if you come up with plausible answers!)

The strategy is of proven effectiveness when the information to be learned concerns familiar concepts. Remember, elaborative techniques help your understanding by relating new information to codes already stored and familiar to you. Thus elaborative interrogation is a strategy best suited to a situation where the information you wish to learn relates to a rich network of information in your database. In other words, elaborative interrogation is effective to the extent that it forces you to construct a better super-cluster.

However, if the underlying concepts themselves are new, elaborative interrogation is of little use (except perhaps to indicate to you the holes in your knowledge!). Elaborative interrogation is useful therefore when you require comprehension as well as recall, but only when you already possess sufficient related knowledge.

Add meaning

As we know, to be memorable information needs to have strong links with accessible codes (potential retrieval cues). Links gain strength from each other, and the best way of encoding information is as a cluster tightly integrated through the sharing of a common theme.

Elaboration is about connecting new information with old. It is about adding meaning. For example, consider the following facts:

> Arteries are thick and elastic and carry blood rich in oxygen from the heart.
>
> Veins are thinner and less elastic and carry blood rich in carbon dioxide back to the heart.

Now, assuming that you know little about anatomy and this information is quite new to you, there are basically three ways you can approach learning this information. The simplest and least effective is to simply rehearse it ad nauseam until firmly entrenched through brute force. A more effective approach would be to use a mnemonic strategy (see chapter nine), which makes arbitrary information more memorable. Thus, for example, you could create memorable sentences such as '*Art*(ery) was *thick* around the middle so he wore pants with an *elastic* waistband.'

However, although this would be helpful if these facts are all the anatomy you wish to acquire, such mnemonics don't help you master anatomy. To develop understanding, you must use a different approach – non-transformational elaboration: building super-clusters.

The critical feature, it is argued, is that you understand the *significance* of the information. Being provided with a raft of additional facts which relate to the information to be learned does not necessarily help – and may indeed hinder memory – if the facts are not directly relevant.

Thus, in our present example, you would ask yourself, why are arteries thicker and more elastic than veins? Does it relate to their different functions? Perhaps arteries need to be elastic because blood is pumped out of the heart in spurts, whereas veins, carrying the blood back to the heart, have less need to be able to expand or contract. (The example is taken from a study by Bransford, Stein, Shelton and Owings.)

Elaborations are effective to the extent that they reduce the arbitrariness of the links between codes. Experts in a field make such elaborations readily. It may well be that this skill is critical in distinguishing successful learners from poor learners.

The poorer your skill at generating effective elaborations, the more you need information to be presented to you with such elaborations spelled out. If you are skilled at seeking out meaningful relationships between facts you will be less affected by the quality of the material presented to you.

Elaborative strategies do require a greater working-memory capacity than a simple strategy such as rehearsal. However, the capacity demands of complex strategies become less as you become more skilled at them.

Exercise 8.4

1. Which is more memorable: 'the donkey *and* the hedge'; 'the donkey *by* the hedge'; or 'the donkey *in* the hedge'?

2. Which list is more memorable?

shell – well	ponce – purse	money – purse
car – star	money – nanny	sand – shell
mouse – house	dress – brass	car – mat
bat – mat	soil – soul	brass – star

Choosing the right study strategy

To decide on the most effective study strategies in a situation where you have meaningful information to understand and remember, you need to first evaluate the information.

We can classify text at one of three different levels, according to its structure and density:

1. simple (straightforward text with clear connections)

2. complex (characterised by many changes of topic and more than one level of information)

3. difficult (dense text with many topic changes, often unclear, inconsistent and/or abstract).

These different types of text require progressively more complex strategies.

Within each level, of course, there are gradations of complexity/difficulty, which also affects your choice of strategy and the number of different strategies you require.

We can classify study strategies into six broad processes:

TYPE OF TEXT	BROAD PROCESSES	SPECIFIC STRATEGIES
Simple	Restating	paraphrasing, visualising, transformational elaboration
Complex	Selecting	underlining, highlighting, boxes, lists
Complex	Abstracting themes	headings, summaries
Complex	Perceiving structure	outlines, graphic organisers
Complex	Making sense of information	elaborative interrogation, analogies, maps, multimedia summaries, restructuring, charts and tables, integrating sections of text
Difficult	Monitoring comprehension	constructing and testing theories about the meaning of the text, seeking additional information

Is the text difficult?

- Assess density: How many different ideas are there in each paragraph? How many on a page?
- Assess the effectiveness of the structure: Is it divided into logical sections? Do the headings encapsulate the themes of the sections? Are changes of theme signalled by headings?
- Look for the presence of effective cues: Are key-points highlighted?
- Assess complexity: Can important concepts be easily conveyed in single words (or brief phrases)? Is the information in each section meaningfully connected? How many changes of theme (topic) are there?
- Compare style: Does the approach match your own?

How *you* learn

Remember, when you evaluate any specific study strategy the critical questions are:

- Does it help you understand the information?
- Does it help you select the important information?

This is a question not simply about the value of a specific strategy in a particular context, but also about *you*. We are all slightly different in the way we approach and perceive information. What works for me won't necessarily work for you. When you choose a strategy, you must also consider your own LEARNING STYLE.

'Learning style' is a term that's bandied around quite a lot, and can mean a variety of things, but here I'm talking about how you approach subjects. Do you simply aim to hammer in the minimum you need to know? Do you rote-learn the essential facts? Do you focus on the words rather than the meaning? These are characteristics of what is termed a SURFACE APPROACH to learning, which involves a superficial processing of information.

You might approach a subject deeply, digging for understanding, trying to make connections that will develop expertise in the subject. Or you might take a middle path, the 'achieving approach', where you aim to do no more than you need to, but you focus on what will be rewarded, managing your time and effort accordingly.

Of course, we all use each one of these approaches at different times and in different situations. Personal interest, the skills and enthusiasm of a particular teacher, and particular subjects, all influence our approach to a learning task.

Physical sciences, for example, tend to emphasise detail, so that a DEEP APPROACH – one that seeks meaning – may superficially be very similar to a surface approach – one that aims simply to reproduce information. However, sciences also require you to understand cause-and-effect relationships, which require a more analytic approach, so you must be careful that you don't get bogged down in too much detail.

Perhaps most of all, these different approaches reflect your motives. Are you studying something because you're interested in it? This intrinsic motivation is, unsurprisingly, associated with a deep approach. Or are you motivated by the need to do well (perhaps to pass an exam, or perhaps to show other people), or even the need not to look like an idiot? Again unsurprisingly, this extrinsic motivation is more likely to be found in cases of a surface approach.

In general, in any subject, a deep approach is a far superior approach if you are intending to acquire a certain level of expertise.

The most effective approach, if your goal is understanding as well as remembering, is searching for the underlying, connecting principles. (Even vocabulary can be understood rather than simply memorised. Few words are arbitrary. If you understand the derivations of words, you are much more likely to remember them.) However, an achieving approach can be nearly as effective as a deep approach, if you have successfully worked out your goals and managed your learning.

The surface approach can be perfectly adequate, however. If your goal is simply to pass exams, then rote-learning is all you need for regurgitating facts (as long as you aren't going to be asked questions that require you to go beyond the information you have been given, and demonstrate that you can draw the right inferences from the underlying concepts and principles you have ostensibly learned). The key, as always, is in your selection of the 'right' information to be memorised.

Students who follow a surface approach are usually mainly concerned with achieving a task and fulfilling its requirements. Such students typically are happy for the teachers to set the learning tasks, and are primarily interested in the qualification they will achieve. Students who are interested in the subject for itself, on the other hand, are more likely to want to play a part in setting their own learning boundaries, and tend to actively dislike examinations and lectures (which reflect the teacher's boundaries).

Whether you take a surface, achieving or deep approach to learning, you will do it in your own way. Cognitive style is your general tendency to process information in a particular way. You may, for example, pay attention to the global features of experiences. Or you may prefer a point-by-point analysis of details (especially enjoying the specification of rules).

There are advantages and disadvantages to both these approaches. Globalists, those who look for the 'big picture', are usually good at seeing things in context, but they may miss important details and are more likely to have trouble selecting what's important. Analytics, on the other hand, are good at detail and good at seeing similarities and differences, but they may focus on one or two aspects to the exclusion of other, equally important aspects.

Analytics like a step-by-step approach, but globalists can get confused by such an approach, particularly when the steps are large. Analytics may find overviews confusing; globalists may be confused without an overview. Analytics tend to prefer to take control of their learning; globalists don't care.

Someone with both a global and a deep approach will tend to search for meaning by organising the material into an integrated whole. A student with an analytic and a deep approach, on the other hand, will search for meaning by analysing isolated items. Someone with both a global and a surface approach will want a ready-made organised whole that they can memorise. A student with an analytic and a surface approach will be happy to memorise isolated items.

Transcending your personal style

A truly flexible strategist has a style that integrates all these approaches. What is critical is not so much what your style is, but its suitability for the style of presentation of the information you have to learn. You learn better when the task matches your style. You need to spend more time on information presented in a manner incompatible with your style. Presenting a long list of principles may be a difficult memory task for analytical students, who try to memorise each relationship. For global learners the same task may tap conceptual reorganisation skill rather than memorisation skill.

Rather than try to *change* your style (a difficult undertaking), you should try to *transcend* it: to be aware of your style, to know its strengths, and, more importantly, to know its weaknesses.

LEARNING STYLE	WEAKNESSES	RECOMMENDED PROCESSES
Deep global	not attending to important details	selecting (highlighting)
Deep analytic	not connecting and integrating information	perceiving structure abstracting themes
Surface global	not seeking underlying relationships and meaning	abstracting themes making sense of information
Surface analytic	not connecting information not seeking underlying relationships and meaning	perceiving structure abstracting themes making sense of information

Remember that your preference for any particular strategy probably reflects your personal style; we're all inclined to like what's easiest for us. But what's easiest is very often not what is best for us! If you want to become a truly successful learner, you need to master those strategies that counteract your weaknesses.

9 Mnemonics - some memory 'tricks'

Aids to memory such as ACRONYMS, rhymes, linking information by creating visual images or making up a story, are called mnemonics. They tend to be regarded as memory 'tricks' rather than memory strategies, but this is being unfair to them. As much as any other memory strategy, mnemonic strategies are built on the basic memory principles.

One reason for the low status of mnemonics is that they are effective for rote memorisation, but of little help in building understanding. However, although understanding is a necessary part of developing expertise, every subject has a core of information that must be learned 'by heart'. And in daily life there are many 'facts' that we need to know, but do not need to understand.

Mnemonic strategies have been recommended as appropriate for remembering the following types of information: vocabulary, names and faces, shopping lists, 'phone numbers, appointments, birthdays and anniversaries, cards, personal numbers (e.g. passport number, bank account number), facts, content of articles or books, speeches, ideas, jokes, dramatic parts and poems.

The limitations of mnemonics are no reason for discarding them. But to use them effectively you must be able to use them *judiciously* – to judge wisely when their use is advised. To do that, you need to understand how the various strategies work.

Imagery mnemonics

Most mnemonic strategies are based on imagery. There is no doubt that imagery can be an effective tool, but there is nothing particularly special about it. The advantage of imagery is that it provides an easy way of connecting information that is not otherwise readily connected. However, providing verbal links (see *Story method*, below) is equally effective.

The critical element is that words or images provide a context which links the information. Thus, imagery is only effective when it is an *interactive* image – one which ties together one bit of information with another. Visual imagery on its own is of limited value without an organising structure, such as the PLACE or PEGWORD METHOD.

It is usually emphasised that bizarre images are remembered much better, but there is no evidence for this. In many studies indeed, ordinary images are remembered slightly better. One of the problems is that people tend to find it harder to create bizarre images. Unless you have a natural talent for thinking up bizarre images, it is probably not worth bothering about.

Exercise 9.1

Here are some items from a visual imagery questionnaire to help you rate your ability to visualise. (The items are taken from Marks' Vividness of Visual Imagery Questionnaire.)

For the following questions, rate your image according to whether it is:

Perfectly clear and as vivid as normal vision	1
Clear and reasonably vivid	2
Moderately clear and vivid	3

Vague and dim	4
No image, you only 'know' that you are thinking of the subject	5

Think of some relative or friend whom you frequently see (but who is not with you at present) and consider carefully the picture that comes before your mind's eye. Rate your image according to the scale on the following points:

1. the exact contour of face, head, shoulders and body
2. characteristic poses of head, attitudes of body, etc.
3. the precise carriage, length of step, etc. in walking
4. the different colours worn in some familiar clothes.

Visualise a rising sun. Consider carefully the picture that comes before your mind's eye.

5. The sun is rising above the horizon into a hazy sky.
6. The sky clears and surrounds the sun with blueness.
7. Clouds. A storm blows up, with flashes of lightning.
8. A rainbow appears.

Add up the total of your rating scores and divide by 8 to give you your average score. An average of over 3 suggests you are a good visualiser, while a score below 2 indicates a poor visualiser.

Making connections

In the previous chapter, I talked about the importance of linking information to be learned with information you already know, and that such connections are achieved through elaboration. I distinguished between transformational elaboration and non-transformational elaboration, and we looked at non-transformational elaboration, which involves abstracting a unifying theme and rewriting the information as an integrated cluster around this theme. In this section, we will look at types of transformational elaboration – ways of making connections which make information more memorable by transforming it into an interactive image.

The keyword method

The KEYWORD METHOD has been especially pushed as an effective strategy for learning foreign vocabulary. It is presumably equally valuable for extending your native-language vocabulary and learning technical jargon, and has also been used successfully to teach social studies facts (e.g. the products of a country, capital cities), science facts (e.g. chemical reactions, parts of the skeletal and nervous systems) and the names and faces of people.

There are two stages to the method. The first is to link the foreign word with an English word that sounds like some part of the foreign word (e.g. the Spanish *carta* sounds like the English *cart*). This (*cart*) is the keyword. The second step involves linking the keyword with the English meaning of the foreign word by forming an interactive image (e.g. *carta* means 'letter', so you could visualise a letter inside a cart).

The keyword method appears to be the most effective means of acquiring vocabularly for comprehension (understanding what a word means when you come across it), but if your goal is an ability to produce the word, rote repetition is better. In other words, your letter in the cart will help you remember what *carta* means when you come across it, but it won't necessarily help you recall the Spanish word for 'letter'.

Similarly, if you learn that Canberra is the capital of Australia by visualising a can on top of a map of Australia, you should find it easy to answer 'What is Canberra the capital of?', but less easy to answer 'What is the capital of Australia?'.

The problem is that, although the keyword component of the word is much more likely to be recalled (the *cart* part of *carta*; the *can* part of *Canberra*), any word with that component seems equally possible.

Think about it. To remember that *carta* means 'letter' you need to:

1. Derive the keyword from the word (*cart* from *carta*).
2. Derive the interactive image from the keyword (*letter in cart* from *cart*).
3. Derive the meaning from the image (*letter* from *letter in cart*).

Although this sounds somewhat complicated, this three-step process is merely repeating the steps by which you originally encoded the information. Clearly, the more obvious your original encoding, the easier it will be to recreate the process (*cart* is an obvious keyword for *carta*; *pet* is not quite so obvious for *pequenos*).

However, to remember the Spanish word for 'letter', you must:

1. Retrieve the interactive image (*letter in cart* from *letter*).
2. Use the image to derive the keyword (*cart* from *letter in cart*).
3. Use the keyword to derive the foreign word (*carta* from *cart*).

While *carta* might seem easily derived from *cart*, other associations are not likely to be so easy – imagine trying to derive *pequenos* from *pet* or *peck*.

The keyword method is very effective for linking a new fact to a well-learned fact, but is little help in recalling the new fact itself. In many cases however, comprehension is the main goal, and in such a case the keyword method is very effective. The main advantage of the keyword mnemonic over other strategies for remembering information of this type is that you acquire the information *faster*, but not better. Learning new words in a meaningful context is an equally effective strategy for long-term recall.

A variant of the keyword method that is used more than other mnemonic strategies is that of FACE-NAME ASSOCIATIONS.

Face-name associations

Because face–name associations are usually only required one way – remembering a name on seeing a face, rather than the other way around – an appropriately modified keyword method would seem potentially more suitable for face–name associations than it is for language learning.

The first step in creating a face–name association is to select a distinctive feature of the face – perhaps the person has a pronounced Roman nose. Now select a word or phrase that sounds like the name (e.g. *con rat* for Conrad). Create an interactive image linking the distinctive feature with the keyword(s), such as a man in a prisoner's uniform (*con*) riding a *rat* that slides down the *nose.*

To remember the name on seeing the face again, you must:

1. Identify the distinctive feature that you used when encoding (*nose*).
2. Use that feature to help you retrieve the interactive image (a *con* riding a *rat* sliding down a *nose*).

3. Derive the keyword(s) from the image (*con rat*).
4. Use the keyword to help you retrieve the name (*Conrad*).

As we have discussed, the connection between a person's name and their looks is entirely arbitrary, which is why the focus of the face–name association strategy is on forging a connection between physical features and the name (via visually derived semantic codes).

The distinctive feature is pivotal to the success of the method. Without a distinctive feature the method doesn't work. The more distinctive the feature, the more effective the method will be. But most faces are not that distinctive! It's hard to select a distinctive feature in many cases, and even harder to find a distinctive feature that you haven't used frequently before.

Most people find the strategy too difficult and time-consuming to apply in most social situations. With a great deal of practice you can of course become skilled at the method. But if you do not have a natural facility for this strategy, and you are not prepared to put in a great deal of practice, you are unlikely to find this a useful strategy for frequent use.

Although not quite so effective, a much easier strategy (which will still considerably improve your recall of people's names) involves simply repeating the person's name as often as you can: when you are introduced, during conversation, and when you say goodbye.

That is not to say that face–name association is not worth having in your toolbox. If remembering people's names is a priority for you, then it is certainly worth putting some time into practising this strategy. Even if you lack the skill to use the strategy regularly, you can still master it sufficiently well for use when remembering a particular name is important enough for you to put in some effort.

However, the main value of the face-name association strategy is in situations where you have a large number of names to learn and peace to learn them. For example, a teacher could use this method to learn the names of all his students on the first day of class (provided he has time to sit quietly and stare at them!). If you are in a situation where you have a large number of names to learn, photographs of the people would enable you to apply this strategy in your own time.

Learning lists

The best-known strategies that employ imagery are the LIST-LEARNING STRATEGIES: the place method, the pegword method, and the LINK METHOD. This type of strategy is trivially useful for shopping lists, and can be useful for learning the right order of items. It can also be used for memorising retrieval cues and anchoring many details. But remember what I said earlier about the difference between making arbitrary rather than meaningful connections: while list-learning strategies can help you learn faster, they won't help you learn *better*.

Also, to be used effectively, all steps need to be properly implemented and – the difficulty for many people – you need to be able to create images quickly.

For all these reasons, while list-learning strategies are undoubtedly effective, they perhaps have less value as general strategic tools than the TRANSFORMATIONAL ELABORATIVE STRATEGIES – the keyword method, and face–name association.

The place method

The place method (the method of loci, as it is traditionally known) is the classic mnemonic strategy, having its first recorded use 2,500 years ago.

First of all, choose a place you know very well. You might use a familiar route, your house, or a particular room in it. The crucial thing is that you can easily call to mind various 'landmarks' (different fixed objects in a room, for example). These landmarks are your anchors. You must train yourself to go around your landmarks in a particular order. With a route of course, that is easy.

To remember a list (say a shopping list) simply imagine each item in turn at these landmarks. For example, a loaf of bread sticking out of the letterbox, a giant apple in place of the door, the hall full of beans, a giant banana in the bath, etc.

This technique is extremely effective for learning lists, not surprisingly, for it obeys two of our fundamental principles:

- it uses over-learned cues to anchor new information
- it uses visual imagery to strengthen the links.

Because the place method uses cues that are already well known to you, it is probably the easiest of the imagery mnemonics to master.

A situation where the place method is particularly appropriate and effective is in the case of waiting staff who go from table to table to take drink orders. Visualising the drinks in particular locations is more effective than writing the orders down, probably because the time pressure in that kind of situation makes an internal strategy more effective than an external one.

The pegword mnemonic

The pegword mnemonic is based on the same sort of idea as the place method, but instead of using locations as cues, it uses numbers. These numbers are transformed into visual images by means of the following simple rhyme: 'One is a bun, two is a shoe, three is a tree, four is a door, five is a hive, six is sticks, seven is heaven, eight is a gate, nine is a line, and ten is a hen.'

The rhyme must be learned by rote until it is over-learned. Accordingly, there is a higher 'cost' to the pegword method than to the place method, where cues already over-learned are used. It does however have an advantage over the place method, in that the items learned are not tied to a particular sequence, and therefore it's not necessary to recall the whole list to retrieve a single item.

The link method

Like the place method and the pegword method, the link method uses visual images to link items together. However, instead of a well-learned structure to anchor the new information, items are linked to each other. For example, to remember our shopping list of bread, apples, beans and bananas, you would form an image of the bread interacting with apples in some way, then another image of apples and beans, then another image bringing beans and bananas together. The items are thus chained together.

Limitations

While these strategies are all effective means of learning lists, they do have a number of problems. All of them are difficult to use if the information is presented to you too quickly. The pegword and link methods in particular are difficult to use effectively without extensive training. If you merely want to recall an item from the list, rather than needing to recall the whole list, both the place and the link methods require you to start from the beginning and go through in order until you reach the item you want. In the case of the place and pegword methods, by using the landmarks again and again, you can only readily recall the last list. Earlier lists are much less easily recalled. The technique is therefore of value only as a relatively short-term memory strategy, not as a way of acquiring permanent knowledge.

Using list-learning mnemonics with other strategies

Mnemonic list-learning strategies have more potential usefulness when used in conjunction with other strategies, because list-learning strategies can do a number of memory-improving things that we have discussed: they can organise information; they can provide anchors for information; and they can strengthen links.

Remembering the emphasis I have placed on the need for anchors (those key bits of information that serve as reference points for a cluster) it will be apparent that mnemonic list-learning strategies have the potential to be an effective means of encoding those anchors for easy recall.

There are two main kinds of textual material for which mnemonic strategies are particularly appropriate:

- text that is readily understandable, but which contains a number of details that might be overlooked
- text that is structured, but is not sufficiently well known or well organised for the structure to be used as a frame for retrieval.

To use a list-learning strategy for text, you need first to understand the information. Then select your anchors: to do this, choose details you suspect you wouldn't otherwise remember, or details that would serve as effective cues for other bits of information. Now encode the anchors using a mnemonic (that is, by creating a visual image for them) and finally cluster the encoded anchors using a list-learning mnemonic (such as the place method).

The use of a mnemonic list-learning strategy in such a manner is of demonstrated effectiveness.

A warning

Mastering a subject requires you to acquire a large number of 'facts' and new vocabulary and accordingly, mnemonic strategies would seem potentially effective means of acquiring these basics. However, being an expert is not simply a matter of 'knowing a lot'. An expert has a well-organised domain into which new information can be easily integrated. Mnemonic techniques on their own do not help you understand the meaning of facts and do not therefore help you develop expertise in a subject.

Verbal mnemonics

The emphasis on visual imagery in mnemonics reflects in part the low level of literacy through most of human history. Today, methods that use words rather than images have been shown to be equally effective among people with higher levels of literacy. Imagery has one major advantage, the ease with which two items can be connected using imagery, but it also has one major disadvantage, the difficulty most people have creating images. Like visual mnemonics, verbal mnemonics come in two types: transformational strategies and list-learning strategies.

Making words

The transformational strategies we looked at earlier make information more memorable by transforming it into an interactive image. In verbal transformational strategies, information is made more memorable by transforming it into words. This is what happens with coding mnemonics.

Coding mnemonics

Coding mnemonics are used for encoding numbers. Because words are much easier for most of us to remember, a system that transforms numbers into letters is one of the best ways for remembering numbers.

Here is one such coding system:

1 = t (there is *1* downstroke in *t*)

2 = n (there are *2* downstrokes in *n*)

3 = m (there are *3* downstrokes in *m*)

4 = r (*r* is the last letter of *four*)

5 = l (*l* is 50 in Roman numbers)

6 = sh (*six* has a sort of *sh* sound)

7 = k (number *7* is embedded in *k*)

8 = f (both *8* and *f* have two loops)

9 = p (*9* is *p* the wrong way round)

0 = s (*zero* starts with a *s* sound)

The codes are not arbitrary. they have been chosen with a view to facilitating rote memorisation. As you can see,however, some of the rationales are somewhat contrived. If you want to have a coding strategy in your toolbox, you are not obliged to memorise a coding system that is given to you. There is no particular superiority in any one set of digit–letter equivalences over another. But if you are modifying a coding system by substituting equivalences you find more obvious, you need to bear in mind confusability. For example, an equivalence between *f* and *5* might seem obvious, but there is a strong likelihood of becoming confused between *4* and *5* when decoding.

Once encoded into letters, the numbers can then be incorporated into words or rhymes. For example, the Second World War ended in 1945 – *tprl*, which could be turned into *top role*. (Only consonants are used for coding; Vowels are then inserted as necessary.)

The modern innovation of encoding phone numbers into letters (0800 ANSETT) is a useful descendent of this strategy.

A coding system is very useful for remembering numbers, but it must be said that few people have sufficient need to memorise long numbers to make the initial cost of learning the code acceptable. There are exceptions of course. You may have a job where the memorisation of many prices, quantities or measurements is required or desirable, for example. But for most of us, written and electronic records are far preferable, being far less costly and more reliable. The advent of smart telephones has of course made a huge difference to our need to memorise phone numbers.

Of course, such records have their disadvantages. They are not always available when you require them, and they may be lost or destroyed. How important those dangers are is a matter for the individual to decide.

The coding system has another value: that of supplying pegs for the pegword system. By allowing numbers to be encoded as easily remembered words, the number of pegs can be extended from ten into infinity. For example, the pegword for 22 could be *nun*. Lists of such pegwords are available in various memory improvement books. Clearly of course, mastery of such a system requires a very large investment of time and effort, as well as a facility for image creation. But if you decide that the pegword strategy is for you, you should certainly increase its value by learning a coding system.

Such systems have been suggested for memorising such information as appointments, and birthdays and anniversaries. There is no evidence that mnemonic strategies are particularly effective for tasks in the planning memory domain and most people find external strategies – diaries, calendars, watch alarms – more dependable and easier to use. Humour is of course replete with instances of people (usually men) forgetting birthdays and anniversaries, but I suspect that any person sufficiently motivated to use a mnemonic strategy for this purpose, would be sufficiently motivated to remember without use of such aids.

The main value of an extended pegword system is to a person who intends to use it regularly as a means of encoding anchors for 'factual' information, or a person who has an unusual need to memorise numbers.

Exercise 9.2

Transform the following into their letter codes and make up a memorable word or phrase:

04 489 6535

21 October 1963

4 p.m. 6 February

0062534 25

Learning lists

As with imagery mnemonics, the best known verbal mnemonics are list-learning strategies. One in particular is familiar to everyone: FIRST-LETTER MNEMONICS (such as ROYGBIV, for the colours in the rainbow) This is an effective means of learning the order of well-learned information in the right circumstances, and has the advantage of being easily learned. However, it is limited in its application. The other list-learning strategy we'll look at is the story method, which is the direct verbal counterpart of the link method.

First-letter mnemonics

First-letter mnemonics are probably the most widely used mnemonic. This reflects the popularity of specific mnemonics, rather than its wide use as a strategic tool.

There are two types of first-letter mnemonic: acronyms, in which the initial letters form a meaningful word – such as FACE for the notes in the spaces of the treble clef – and ACROSTICS, in which the initial letters are used as the initial letters of other words to make a meaningful phrase – such as *E*very *G*ood *B*oy *D*eserves *F*ruit, for the notes on the lines of the treble staff.

Medical students tend to rely heavily on such mnemonics to help them master anatomical details, such as the names of the cranial nerves: On Old Olympia's Towering Top A Finn And German Vault And Hop (olfactory, optic, oculomotor, trochlear, trigeminal, abducens, facial, auditory, glossopharyngeal, vagus, accessory and hypoglossal). This demonstrates the major limitation of this method; its value is entirely in serving as a reminder of information that is already very well-learned. Learning 'On Old Olympia's Towering Top A Finn And German Vault And Hop' would not help most of us remember the cranial nerves, because the nerves themselves are not sufficiently familiar to us. ROYGBIV helps us recall the colours of the spectrum, in the correct order, because the names of the colours are already well known to us.

Learning a first-letter mnemonic does not help you learn the information being cued by the mnemonic. For the mnemonic-phrase to be an effective cue, the information being cued must be well learned.

This brings us to the chief use of this method. First-letter mnemonics are a very effective means of recalling the *order* of well-learned items. First-letter mnemonics are a cueing strategy: they remind us of what we already know. They are therefore particularly effective as a means to overcome memory blocks; for example, for students whose minds 'go blank' in exams.

They can, of course, lead to errors when more than one item shares the same first letter. The acrostic for cranial nerves, for example, contains three Os, two Ts and two As! As with image formation, some people find it harder to think up acrostics than others. (One student reportedly took 20 minutes to make up one six-letter phrase!)

The story method

The story method is another list-learning strategy. It is the verbal equivalent of the link method. Items are chained together by linking them in a story. For example, here is a story created by a participant in an experiment, in order to remember some arbitrary items (italicised): A *vegetable* can be a useful *instrument* for a *college* student. A carrot can be a *nail* for your *fence* or *basin*. But a *merchant* of the Queen would *scale* that fence and feed the carrot to a *goat*.

The story method is as effective as the imagery methods for learning lists. Which one will be most effective for you depends on which type of information (words or images) you deal with most easily.

When should you use mnemonics?

Traditionally, education has involved the rote memorisation of facts. In modern times this focus has been (justly) deplored, and emphasis has been placed instead on the importance of *understanding* information. As is common with revolutions, the reaction has perhaps been excessive. It is not true that all information is meaningful. It is not true that only information that can be understood is worth learning. My father's birthday is worth my while learning, but it is not meaningful. There is no meaning between a person's name and their face. The colour-coding of electric wires is not something that can be understood.

Certainly information that is meaningful should be learned in a meaningful way, but information which is not meaningful or integrated (or potentially so) needs to be learned in a different way. The principles of learning, however, apply to all information. Meaning and organisation always aid recall. Effective retrieval cues are always critical. To improve your recall of unrelated information, therefore, you need to find some way of supplying meaning, organisation and effective cues. Mnemonics can provide a structure on which to anchor information and connect otherwise unrelated information.

But the cost of most mnemonic strategies is high: higher for some people than others. For most tasks, there are less costly strategies which, though perhaps less effective, are sufficiently effective to be preferable for many people. The principal alternatives to mnemonic strategies are: written or electronic records, and rote repetition. For many tasks and for most people, a written list is far less effort, far more likely to be used and far more reliable.

Some people feel that they are unable to use a list effectively because they always forget to take it. However, research has confirmed what many of us already know from experience: even if you forget to take your list, you are much more likely to recall items that you have written down. The act of writing (and perhaps the opportunity to visualise your list) are sufficient to improve your memory.

The chief advantage of a mnemonic strategy over the much less costly alternative of writing a list is that it can help you remember the items that you recall at times when writing materials are not available (such as while driving). This is why proponents of mnemonic strategies sometimes suggest that mnemonics can help you remember ideas. More than most types of information, ideas are something that often come to us in situations where writing down is not an option, or at least inconvenient – in bed, out walking, in a car, talking to someone.

One of the more valuable uses of a mnemonic list-learning strategy is as an aid to remembering a speech or presentation. A mnemonic strategy has three main advantages over the preferred alternative strategy of written notes: written notes can be lost or left behind; looking down at written notes breaks your rapport with the audience; referring to written notes can break your flow.

Mnemonics have also sometimes been suggested as an aid to remembering dramatic parts. Information such as this needs to be remembered verbatim, and there is no real substitute for rote repetition. However, some people have found mnemonic list-learning strategies helpful as an adjunct to this strategy, to provide them with retrieval cues signalling what comes next. Mnemonic strategies are of course excellent for the purpose of signalling the order of well-learned information.

Looking at our list of ten memory tasks, we can see that mnemonic strategies can be useful in half those tasks. They are not, as a general rule, particularly appropriate for information in the planning memory domain, or the event memory domain. In the case of the first task (remembering information you have studied), mnemonic strategies are most useful as an adjunct to other strategies.

Choosing the right mnemonic

WHAT DO YOU WANT TO REMEMBER?	WHICH MNEMONIC?
information you have studied	keyword method; list-learning strategies
someone's name/face	face–name associations
important dates	coding mnemonic
the names of things	keyword method
how to do something	list-learning strategies

Exercise 9.3

Read the following descriptions of some memory situations, and choose an appropriate mnemonic strategy.

1. You're a sales representative and you want to impress your customers by remembering the details of previous purchases without referring to a piece of paper. What memory strategy do you use?
2. You ring directory enquiries from a public phone box, then find the number you want is engaged and you will have to remember it for several minutes, if not longer. You are without anything to write with. What do you use to remember it?
3. You are going to a function at your partner's workplace and you ask your partner to remind you of the names and roles of the various people she works with. How do you remember them?

4. You're a waiter and want to remember what the people at various tables have ordered without constantly referring to your list. What strategy do you use?

5. Your boss calls you over and gives you a number of instructions. How do you ensure you remember them all?

10 Improving your attention

We have spent a lot of time looking at understanding and selecting information. It is time we looked at the third leg of our tripod: attention.

Instead of manipulating information to make it easier to remember, general support strategies manipulate your ability to process information. They do this primarily through their effect on your attention. There are two aspects to improving attention: the first is about improving the *quality* of your attention; the second is about improving the *direction* of your attention.

Although everyone agrees that 'paying attention' is critical in improving your learning and remembering, there is very little evidence for it. This is partly because no one really understands what attention is, and, relatedly, because the effectiveness of training programmes to improve attentiveness has not been properly assessed.

The following elements have been suggested as important in improving the quality and focus of your attention:

- eliminating distractions (external and internal)
- limiting how long you concentrate for
- setting deadlines
- establishing goals
- increasing motivation.

Remembering that we are limited in the amount of information we can work with at one time, I would add to this list:

- limiting the amount of information you try to process at one time.

Let's look first at those strategies designed to direct your attention appropriately. Remember, however well you are concentrating, it does little good if you are attending to the wrong information!

Set yourself goals

Goal-setting is fundamental to effective encoding. You can't choose the right strategy, or appropriately direct your attention, or effectively manage your time, unless you know exactly what your goal is.

There are two aspects to setting goals wisely. The first relates to how well you articulate your goal, the second to the type of goal. I have already defined the fundamental principle of effective goal-setting (in the context of effective retrieval searches):

Be specific

Not only is it easier to assess whether you have defined your goal accurately when you have defined it specifically, but it is also easier to judge whether the goal is realistic. Thus, aiming to learn all the faces and names of the people at your new workplace within a week is a much better goal than aiming to 'get better at putting names to faces'.

In specifying your goal, it helps if you also establish what you *don't* need to know. This helps limit your search, and allows you to focus on what you do need to know.

Part of specifying your goal concerns the level of mastery you want to achieve. For example, you might only want to learn enough to pass a test. The level of mastery depends also on how long you want to remember the information for. If the test is the next day, you will put in less effort than if the test is next week. Similarly, if you simply want to remember the names of people at your partner's workplace long enough not to embarrass yourself at a particular fuction, you will adopt a different strategy than if you want to remember their names for an indefinite period.

Break it down

Goals may be either PROCESS GOALS, or OUTCOME GOALS. As its name suggests, an outcome goal defines your objective in terms of achieving a particular outcome (e.g. to learn to drive a car, to read a chapter, to spend four hours studying). Process goals refer to specific steps on the way to achieving that outcome (thus a process goal for learning to drive a car might be to learn to start the car smoothly).

In general, process goals appear to be more effective than outcome goals. However, the best strategy seems to be to work towards process goals in the early stages of learning a skill, but once the components have been mastered, to work towards an outcome goal.

For example, in a study of dart throwing, novices who were told to concentrate on properly executing the last two (specified) steps in every throw, did better than those who were told to concentrate on achieving a high numeric score. But the most accomplished novices were those who were first told to concentrate on those process goals and then, when they had mastered those, were told to concentrate on achieving a high score. Not only did this flexible strategy result in better mastery of the skill, but also greater interest and satisfaction. Similarly, successful writers and academics (who tend to have long deadlines and little feedback) often use sub-goals such as daily output charts to help them work towards a distant outcome goal such as finishing a book.

Part of the reason for the greater effectiveness of process goals may simply relate to their greater specificity. Specificity may also be the reason why the use of process goals seems to result in users being less likely to see poor performance as due to a lack of ability. Instead they (rightly) see it as a failure to master a particular skill, probably through insufficient practice.

Setting a number of process goals also gives you intermediate objectives that can provide a framework for a system of small rewards to yourself.

Exercise 10.1

What is your goal in reading this book? Can you specify the sub-goals you have developed during the course of reading this book (e.g. to master the face–name association strategy) and the specific steps you will need to perform (e.g. to think up distinctive features for a specified set of people)? Are these process goals specific enough that you will recognise when you have achieved them?

Manage your time

One characteristic of less successful students is that they tend not to appropriately manage their time. Instead of allocating time on the basis of the difficulty of the information to be learned, they tend to spend *more* time on material that is easier to understand,

and *less* time on material that is difficult. Successful learners, on the other hand, are much better at assessing the difficulty of material, and appropriately managing their efforts.

Effective learners commonly use specific strategies for managing their study time, such as scheduling a regular time for study, setting specific output goals, and using ENVIRONMENTAL AIDS such as watches, alarms and appointment books.

How long does it take?

Before starting a learning task, note down the following:

- How much time do you think the task will take?
- What steps are involved in reaching the goal?

At the end of the task, answer the following:

- Did you have enough time? Too much time?
- Was the task more complex than you had thought?
- How would you approach a similar task in the future?

After you have done this a number of times, you will start to develop a better sense of what goals and time-frames are realistic.

The actual level of your goal is an important determinant of how long you spend studying: someone aiming for a 90 per cent pass in a test usually spends a lot longer than someone just 'doing their best'. But while it is important to *manage* your time, time should not be used as a goal, for example, by saying that you will spend four hours studying. To use your time wisely, it must be considered in conjunction with process and outcome goals.

To develop your time-management skills, you first have to become aware of how you spend your time. Keeping a log of your activities at 30-minute intervals for a week is usually a real eye-opener! Then you need to develop a realistic appreciation of how much you can achieve in a particular time-period.

To effectively manage your time, you need to set specific and realistic goals, and realistic time allotments.

Monitor your progress

There are a number of strategies you can use to monitor how well you're handling the learning process. The most common are testing strategies (testing recall, or testing recognition by matching answers to initial questions), and revising strategies (such as redrafting or recalculation). They also include strategies such as checking performance against goals, and setting revised goals.

A critical factor behind effective learners' superior time management skills is in fact their better monitoring skills. If you don't realise that you haven't learned something adequately (and this is frequently true), then you are unlikely to devote any more time to it.

In most cases, people stop studying long before they have reached the desired level of mastery of the material. There are a number of reasons for this:

- a faulty knowledge of how long it takes to properly incorporate new information
- failure to properly check recall
- failure to understand the material without realising they don't understand
- lack of time
- lack of motivation.

Part of the problem people have with knowing how long it will take them to properly encode some particular information is their poor judgement of how difficult the information is. Like any other skill, judging item difficulty is a skill that needs well-directed practice.

Perhaps because the difficulty of specific items is much easier to judge than the difficulty of broad ideas, your awareness of how well you know something tends to be better for specific details.

An important component of monitoring your learning is testing your memory. While people are very consistent about their judgements of what information they hold in store ('I can't remember it right now, but I know I know it'), they are not actually very accurate, particularly when the information is difficult. Thus your opinion that you have learned something is not, in itself, worth a great deal.

Even people who trouble to test their memory for newly-encoded information do not necessarily do it right. For example, if you test your *recognition* of the information rather than your ability to *recall* it, you will get an inflated idea of how much you know. Less obviously, if you test your recall too soon after encoding you will also over-rate your grasp of the information. To adequately test whether new information has been properly incorporated into your database, you need to try and recall it some considerable time later.

You can monitor either time or goals. Monitoring time can have a hindering effect, however, by diverting attention away from what, after all, is far more important: what you have accomplished, not how long you stared at your books. Monitoring performance on specific goals, by directing attention appropriately, is usually better.

Goal-setting, time-management and monitoring cannot be considered independent of each other. Efficient time-management involves setting realistic goals. Realistic goal-setting requires you to take the amount of time available into consideration. Monitoring is at its best when it measures performance against both time and goals.

Your monitoring skills are not determined by your general competence, nor by your expertise in a particular area, but they are likely to be affected by your personality. Impulsive people, in particular, are likely to be poor at monitoring.

Control your environment

Your environment can affect your remembering in several different ways. You'll remember, in the first part of this book, we saw how it was easier to remember something when we were in the same place as when we originally encountered it. The context effect points to the value of trying to match the retrieval environment with the environment in which you originally encoded the information.

The environment itself can of course also affect learning, as anyone who rails at teenagers for doing their homework with music blaring understands. Structuring your environment for better concentration is particularly beneficial for people with a lower working memory capacity, but there are no hard and fast rules about what constitutes a good environment. Some people, for example, find a certain level of background noise helps them concentrate, whereas others need complete quiet. Extremes of temperature also impair memory, but within those limits there will be a temperature range that is optimal for *you*. What is important is that a) you structure your environment to suit *you*, and b) you use that environment consistently.

The environment is also a potential source of strategies, in the form of environmental aids which can cue recall, such as:

- entering appointments in a diary or on a calendar
- writing on the back of your hand
- using clocks, oven timers, alarms on watches, etc.
- putting objects in a conspicuous place
- tying a knot in your handkerchief.

Using such aids is particularly helpful when a number of interfering activities occur between encoding and recall (for example, having to remember to buy groceries after work), or when there is a long time between encoding and recall (for example, needing to make a doctor's appointment two months in the future). They are also useful in circumstances when internal aids are not trusted to be sufficiently reliable, as when precise details need to be remembered, or strict timing is required – when to check a cake in the oven, for example. Environmental aids reduce the need for working memory, so they are also good when memory load is to be avoided, such as when you are attending to more than one activity.

Social situations

Perhaps the most difficult situation for encoding and retrieving information is conversation with other people. Here are some tips for dealing with this situation:

- restate what has just been said
- keep the conversation to a narrow focus
- slow the rate at which information is presented
- ask questions (to gain time)
- ask questions (to elaborate information)

Control yourself

While your genes clearly have a part to play in decreeing how well you can pay attention, your attentional abilities are far from cast in stone. Most of us change over time in how well we can concentrate, but this isn't solely down to age (although that plays a part). There are a number of mental and physical factors that can affect our attention.

Physical condition

In the main, improving your memory by improving your physical condition is about eliminating habits that impair memory. Your mind works better if you eat properly (not too much; not too little; the right sort of food) and get some exercise. It works better if not impaired by substances such as alcohol, tobacco, marijuana, some tranquillisers and sedatives. Whether you can actually improve memory by becoming super-fit and healthy is much less clear.

A rather more interesting aspect of physical condition effects (because it doesn't depend on will power!) concerns sleep and your daily biological rhythm. Research has found that remembering is markedly worse in the first 20 minutes after waking, but otherwise the time of day doesn't affect your ability to retrieve information from the database. However, in general, encoding (putting information into memory) is better done in the afternoon or evening (although morning may be a better time for older adults). This may be due to an increased ability to concentrate.

Emotional state

Intense emotion, depression or stress can impair memory, probably by making it more difficult to concentrate. While there is no evidence that using relaxation or meditation techniques as a matter of routine has any effect on learning (various claims notwithstanding), specific relaxation techniques (not simply telling yourself to relax!) can help on occasions when you are stressed or anxious.

As I have mentioned earlier, mood can also affect memory through its role in context. If your mood when retrieving matches that obtaining when you originally encoded the information, it will be easier to recall the information.

Attitude

As touched on in chapter one, you perform better when you believe in yourself and your skills. A person who believes they have a good memory already has an advantage over someone who believes they have a poor memory, regardless of how true those beliefs are.

Attitude can also affect your *selection* of information. We are less inclined to remember information that we disagree with or are uncomfortable with. We are more inclined to remember information that supports prejudices and beliefs we hold.

11 Think strategically

The main difficulty in improving your memory is not the learning of specific memory strategies, but in learning which strategy is appropriate to use on a particular task.

You can acquire knowledge about when to use specific strategies through instruction, but you need to go beyond this. You need to develop your own rich knowledge of when different strategies work for you, by:

1. comparing strategies with each other
2. assessing which is most effective in particular memory situations
3. remembering this information for later use.

A good strategy user is one who first analyses the task, noting similarities and differences with other tasks, then assesses which strategies are most likely to be effective. Methodically trying out appropriate strategies, they monitor each one's performance to determine whether it is indeed effective.

Match the task to a strategy

To choose an appropriate strategy we need to understand the nature of the memory task. For example, outlining is an effective strategy when dealing with an expository text such as this one, but it wouldn't be useful if you were wanting to remember a folk tale. Answering questions embedded in the text appears to help you remember a folk tale, but not (oddly enough) an expository text.

Often, of course, more than one memory strategy is required in a situation. Thus, in encoding text, you might use summarisation and elaboration, as well as a mnemonic strategy for specific details such as names.

The emphasis throughout most of this book has been on encoding – and rightly, because it is only through encoding effectively that you will achieve serious memory improvement. However, we must never forget that encoding and retrieving are reflections of each other. When you retrieve information, your strategy must match the strategy used when the information was encoded.

Thus, if you originally learned the material using rhymes, then a rhyme cue is most likely to be effective. Similarly, if you are trying to remember an autobiographical event, it is best to search for those sorts of cues that usually mark such events: cues of activity, place and people present.

The following table suggests appropriate strategies (some specific and some broad principles) for common memory tasks:

MEMORY TASK	APPROPRIATE STRATEGIES
information you have studied	study strategies; keyword method; mnemonic list-learning strategies
someone's name/face	attending to distinctive and unchangeable features; conversational strategies; face–name associations
important dates	coding mnemonic; external aids
details about another person	building strong links between structural and biographical codes, and between biographical codes and related clusters
to do something	external aids; encoding trigger events
when/where something happened	encoding distinctive features
whether you've done something	paying attention
where you've put something	paying attention
names of things	keyword method; repetition; seeking the meaning of names
how to do something	practice; list-learning strategies; external aids

Become a strategic thinker

Being a successful strategist requires more than a knowledge of good strategies and more than knowing when to use them (although these are both important). You need to become a strategic thinker.

A strategic thinker automatically sees a memory situation as requiring a strategy. For example, say you heard on the car radio that the stock market had fallen 14 points, that the FTSE 100 index was 5440.20, and that the pound had fallen to US$1.42. Say you want to remember these details.

The naive memoriser would probably repeat these numbers over and over again, and because there are too many numbers, and you are engaged in another task (driving a car), would almost certainly lose most if not all of the information.

A person with some knowledge of mnemonic strategies might try to chunk the digits in a meaningful way, but unless they are particularly skilled at this will also probably lose much of the information, again because of the complexity of the information, the small amount of time you have to encode the information, and the fact that you are engaged in another task.

A strategic thinker, on the other hand, would instantly realise the problems they are up against, and just as quickly identify the strategies needed to deal with the situation. They would then decide whether they possess the required internal strategy at the requisite level of skill (quite high in the particular circumstances), and if so, they would be employing it before the first number had finished.

The point is, in many common situations, your time to encode information is extremely limited. You do not have the luxury to sit and ponder and consult your notes. You must recognise instantly:

1. that you wish to remember something
2. what information, exactly, you wish to remember
3. the constraints of the situation
4. whether you in fact possess the requisite skills given the constraints of the situation
5. which strategy is appropriate.

In the above situation, a strategic thinker would have realised as soon as the stock market report had come on, that they would need to remember a number of figures. They would have realised that they would have very little time to encode the figures, and that their attention would be divided. They would have probably decided that a pegword mnemonic would be the most appropriate strategy for encoding the numbers, and if they were confident of their mastery of this particular strategy, would have brought it to the forefront of their mind ready to use it. On the other hand, if they realised their skill was insufficient in the circumstances, they might have decided to follow an alternative strategy: pull over, and dig out a pen and paper. The point is, that they made all these decisions almost instantly, because they were mentally prepared, and practised at analysing memory situations.

The first step in becoming a strategic thinker then, is practising your appraisal of memory situations. As with all memory strategies, you need to practise this strategy until its use is habitual and automatic if you want to achieve durable memory improvement.

How much information?

The most important part of improving your memory is recognising that you can't remember everything. The key to successful remembering is selecting what you need to remember. You need to develop your ability to recognise just how much information you can take away from a particular situation.

To estimate how much information you should select, you need to consider:

- the rate of presentation
- the style of the information
- the density of the information
- your level of related knowledge.

Assess the memory situation

The memory situation is something rather more than the memory task, although of course it includes the memory task. For example, imagine that you have called directory enquiries for a long-distance number, from a public phone.

The task is an encoding one. It concerns remembering a number, which is eleven digits long. The first five digits are meaningful (representing the area code, which you probably know). The other six digits are not meaningful. The number is given to you aurally, once only. Your goal is to remember the number long enough to dial it. You have no need to remember it beyond that point. But you must remember it exactly. You are alone in a public place. You have no means of writing a number down, and you have nobody available to help you remember the number.

On the basis of this analysis (which sounds long and complicated, but in fact is no more than we do many times daily without thinking – the difference is that these points are rarely made explicit), you will realise that our choice of strategies is between a mnemonic coding strategy and simple maintenance rehearsal. Unless you are very skilled at coding numbers, you will most probably opt for maintenance rehearsal.

However, if the situation changes – the line is engaged and you have to remember the number for longer – you may reconsider your alternatives. If you can devise a mnemonic for the number (while holding it in working memory), you may now choose to do that. Or you may decide the most sensible thing is to go in search of a pen (while holding the number in working memory via rehearsal).

When you analyse a task, the first thing you need to recognise is whether it's a matter of encoding or retrieval (this should be very obvious!), and the second is to work out which memory domain is involved (for example, knowledge memory or autobiographical memory). You need to decide whether the information is meaningful or not, and you need to note how the information is presented (e.g. written text, spoken text, pictures, actions).

Assessing the memory situation also requires you to specify your goal. You need to work out what you want the information for, how long you need to remember it for (five minutes, a week, forever?), and how much detail you need.

You also need to note the constraints of context. Are you under time pressure? Are you alone or in a social or group setting? Is your state of mind favourable to attention? Are there environmental constraints (for example, a particularly noisy environment)?

Exercise 11.1

Analyse the following memory situations in terms of the parameters described above, then use that information to decide on an appropriate strategy.

1. You go out with your family to do your Christmas shopping, and realise that you have forgotten your list.
2. The library tells you that you have not returned a book, and you try to recall whether you did or not.
3. You want to make sure you remember your appointment at the dentist.
4. You're reading a book about memory and want to remember the main points.

You will notice that many of the parameters of a memory situation do not really apply to retrieval tasks. For a retrieval task, the main concerns are a) what type of information it is (what memory domain is involved), and b) relevant aspects of the retrieval context.

Think through a situation

A strategic thinker, as we have seen, doesn't stop thinking strategically once she's decided on her strategy. A strategic thinker monitors her learning and, if necessary, tries different strategies.

The overall process takes the following steps:

1. Specify the goal.
2. Analyse the task.

3. Choose a strategy.
4. Monitor its performance.
5. Switch strategies if it isn't working.

Your personal style

Effective strategy use is more difficult for those who are habitually impulsive. Such people tend to stop too soon when collecting evidence and often fail to take critical information into account. Thoughtful consideration is required to be a successful strategist. Nor does it help if you are habitually anxious. Strategy planning requires quite a lot of working memory; anxious people reduce their working memory capacity by using some of it for emotional information (thinking negatively about themselves, for example).

This should certainly not be taken to mean that you cannot become a strategic thinker if you are naturally impulsive or anxious. Rather, it should be taken as a warning that personal characteristics need to be taken into account. If you tend to rush into things, you may have to work a little harder to inculcate strategic habits. If you are anxious, or tend to clutter up your mental working space with negative or distracting thoughts, you need to spend some time and effort on strategies that help improve the quality of your attention.

While personal style affects your learning, the most important factors in whether or not you adopt and persist with good memory strategies are:

- your knowledge of how memory works
- your faith in yourself and the strategies.

Put it into practice

Whether you improve your memory is not determined by how intelligent you are, how educated you are, or how old you are. It is determined by your understanding and your mastery of effective memory strategies. Mastery is achieved through practice in different situations. Understanding is achieved by grasping the fundamental principles of how memory works and seeing how they apply to those strategies.

If you have read this book diligently you should now understand the basic principles of how memory works, and – most importantly – see how they underlie effective memory strategies.

If you understand *why* specific strategies are effective, you will know *when* they will be effective. And you will have confidence in them.

But it is not enough to be convinced of a strategy's effectiveness.

Balancing cost with reward

Cost (in time and effort) is a major reason why strategies of known effectiveness are so little used. Cost is determined not only by the demands of the strategy itself, but also by how well you have practised the strategy. The less well you learn a strategy, the more time and effort it will take to apply it. On the other hand, even a basically costly strategy (one that takes considerable time to master) will become much less demanding if sufficiently well practised.

People's use of external memory aids is an example of the principle that cost is often more important than effectiveness.

These are the most frequently used memory strategies:

- writing calendar or diary notes
- putting things in a special place
- writing reminder notes
- writing shopping lists
- using face–name associations
- mentally rehearsing information
- using a timer
- asking someone else to help.

All but two are external memory aids. Why? Not because they're most effective; because they are easy to use.

What are the preferred internal strategies? Mentally retracing (a retrieval strategy) and mentally rehearsing (an encoding strategy): not the most effective strategies, but the least costly. Asking someone to help you remember is also a popular strategy – somewhat to the surprise of researchers – but its popularity is readily understandable. It may not be particularly effective, but it is the least costly strategy of all!

Older people in particular are less inclined to use a strategy merely because it is effective. For them it is far more important that a strategy be familiar and easy to use (i.e. not cost much).

Choose what to remember

This book is not primarily a describer of specific memory strategies, although a number of strategies have been discussed. There are many books which describe specific strategies. The role of this book is to teach you to be a *user of strategies*.

The key to being a successful user is to be a strategic thinker, and for that, you must develop an *awareness* of memory. Get into the habit (develop the skill) of asking yourself: Is this worth remembering? When you're reading the paper: 'Do I want to remember this?' When your partner tells you something: 'Do I need to remember this?' When you meet a new person: 'Do I want to remember this person?'

This sounds rather cold-blooded, but the developing of this awareness is critical to improving your memory. You need to *attend* to encode effectively. (Just don't ask the questions out loud!)

- **Decide** what tasks you are interested in improving.
- **Look** at the strategies appropriate for that particular task.
- **Choose** which strategies suit *you*.
- **Practise** those strategies on varying tasks until you can do them without thinking.
- **Master** one task before going on to the next!

Our world today is increasingly complex and busy. The demands on memory are far greater than they have ever been. And we all feel inadequate in the face of these demands.

Don't!

Forgetting is not a sign of stupidity, nor a sign of growing old. Forgetting is sensible. Don't aim to remember everything; focus on remembering what is important.

And when you do forget something that is important, don't say, 'My mind's going', 'I'm hopeless', 'I can't remember anything'. Say, 'I should have encoded that information better', and learn from your mistake.

Quick reference 1: Tests of working memory capacity

These tests are included for your interest, to give you an idea of your working memory span. Because they are not being administered in controlled conditions, you should not regard them as definitive.

Digit span

This test of your working memory capacity for digits requires the involvement of another person. The tester reads out each sequence of digits, one sequence at a time, at a rate of one digit per second. The person being tested then repeats the sequence back. Some sequences have five digits, some six, and so on up to eight. There are six sequences of each number of digits. The second three of each series should be repeated back in *reverse* order.

Series of five digits:

4 7 9 1 2

8 3 5 2 4

6 2 4 7 1

to be repeated back in reverse order:

9 0 2 5 7

1 6 3 8 5

5 4 0 3 6

Series of six digits:

2 9 8 4 3 1

7 1 6 9 0 8

3 8 1 6 9 0

to be repeated back in reverse order:

0 5 7 1 8 3

9 2 0 3 4 7

4 7 2 0 5 9

Series of seven digits:

1 6 4 8 2 5 3

5 0 3 7 1 2 6

8 3 7 5 6 4 0

to be repeated back in reverse order:

6 4 5 2 7 1 9

4 1 8 3 5 7 2

3 9 0 4 8 6 1

Series of eight digits:

2 5 9 0 3 8 4 7

0 7 1 6 9 3 5 4

9 2 6 1 0 5 8 3

to be repeated back in reverse order:

7 8 2 9 4 0 3 6

1 4 0 5 7 2 9 8

5 9 3 4 1 6 7 2

An average adult can repeat correctly two or three sequences of seven digits. An above-average adult can repeat correctly a sequence of eight digits, and say in reverse order a sequence of seven or more.

Word span

The tester reads out the following words, one set at a time, at a rate of one word per second. The person being tested then repeats the sequence back. Initially the sets have two words. The number of words in a set increases steadily to seven. Stop when you reach the point at which you are unable to recall all words in the correct order, for all three sets of the same size. The level at which you were correct for two of the three sets is the measure of your word span.

stairs meat
wheel hour
tea fire

bread lawn shoe
house book egg
moth cheese spoon

time plate milk deer
floor port thing map
soup wall heart dog

duck cash hand roof train
bed knife day nose shirt
ear bus jam man shelf

cake door fog mouse skirt week
wife pea socks month goose car
bath cup horse oil son work

bank	dress	fruit	love	room	year	wasp
wine	suit	pig	lamp	hair	beach	clock
bean	cow	light	hat	thief	day	pain

Spans for American college students ranged from 4 to 6.

Reading span

The following sentences are to be read aloud, one sentence at a time (cover the text above and below so that you can't see the sentences you have read or the ones you are about to read). At the end of a set, you need to try and recall the last word of each sentence.

> The car turned into the drive and they saw the house for the first time.
>
> She came across the room and bent to pick up the dress discarded on the floor.

> The pig grunted noisily, then heaved itself to its feet and came across to the wall.
>
> He wondered when the van would get here so that he could start work.

> In the morning no tracks could be seen in the heavy dew that blanketed the grass.
>
> Long ago there were kauris here, and now there is only the road.

She was lost in the sky and the balloon was coming down at a frightening speed.

The fog was thick and the crane was a spectral shadow in the ominous silence.

The wine was pleasant but she wondered what would happen when it had been drunk.

Down among the reeds edging the lake he found the limp body of his dog.

On a clear day you could see right across the valley to the swamp.

The boy noticed that the duck seemed to have no fear of people.

He washed up on the beach two days after the worst storm in living memory.

The apples were particularly crisp and went very nicely with the spicy cheese.

The words ran into each other and the room began to spin around him.

The violinist bowed to the audience who applauded madly and stamped their feet.

For many months the crayfish walk right around the islands along the seabed.

He advanced upon the trembling animal, the knife gleaming in his massive hand.

When we heard the bells ring, our first thought was relief that it had finally happened.

She climbed to the top, then stood poised on the very edge of the cliff.

Lost in his memories he stepped out blindly right into the path of the truck.

The little girl asked the teacher whether she could go out and play.

The paper was very gloomy about the possibility of prices rising to an all-time high.

The room was tidy and the bed was made but crayon marked the walls.

He set the table carefully and stepped back to admire the effect of the silver candles.

On the day the wall collapsed I was busy tidying the garden for the party.

The bus stopped with a screech and the old man furiously waved his stick.

The water was calm as a millpond and the sails hung limply on the yachts.

She picked up the phone and paused to consider the stain on the carpet.

The shop was packed with hysterical customers on the first day of the annual sale.

The light plane seemed to hang in the air for a heart-stopping moment.

In the evening the mosquitos came out and whined tirelessly around the fire.

The supermarket trolley spun out of her hands and careered into the old lady.

The boss came in late and snapped at the offer of a cup of coffee.

Oranges and lemons were piled in pyramids on the stalls and glowed in the sun.

When the train arrived five minutes early the waiting passengers all checked the clock.

The chocolate poured out, thick and luscious, over the mound of soft berries.

In the days before cars far more people knew how to ride a horse.

Listening at the keyhole he heard the soft tap of her heels cross the floor.

The river was rising fast but soon they would have all the furniture in the attic.

As the thief ran desperately along the narrow plank, he dropped the jar.

For the last time the ship sailed into the harbour and waited for the small boats.

Among American college students (presumably 'above average' in terms of reading comprehension), reading spans range from 2 to 5.5. High span is defined as 4 and above; medium span as 3–3.5; low as below 3.

Quick reference 2: Glossary

accessible: a memory code is accessible when it is readily activated.
acoustic: the sound of a word.
acronym: uses the initial letters of a list of items to form a meaningful word (e.g. FACE for the notes in the spaces of the treble clef).
acrostic: uses the initial letters of a list of items as the initial letters of other words to make a meaningful phrase (e.g. *E*very *G*ood *B*oy *D*eserves *F*ruit for the notes on the lines of the treble clef).
activate: make a memory code active – to raise its energy level so that it becomes available to you.
active: the state in which a memory code can be looked at and worked with.
active reading: strategies that promote the effective selection of important information by encouraging active involvement in the reading process.
alphabet search: a generation strategy which uses the letters of the alphabet as recall cues.
associative stage: the second stage in the process of learning a skill, in which action steps become coordinated and their sequence learned.
autobiographical memory: a component of personal memory. The memory domain that holds information about yourself, and in particular, about the events and experiences that have happened to you.
autonomous stage: the final stage in the process of learning a skill,

in which the action sequence has become so well-learned that it no longer requires verbal reminders.

biographical codes: another term for semantic codes, to more clearly distinguish semantic codes from visually derived semantic codes.

bit: the smallest amount of information possible. A memory code is made up of a number of bits.

causal chain: the bones of a story: a string of causal connections from the protagonist's goal to the outcome.

chunk: a tight cluster of information identified by a pronounceable label and able to be treated as a single unit when worked with.

clustering: connecting memory codes with many strong links, to the extent that activation of any one code will automatically activate all codes in the cluster.

code: information that has been manipulated and transformed by discarding some bits, and emphasising others.

context: the information contained in the situation in which you are encoding or retrieving the target information. It includes the physical environment and your own physical, mental and emotional state, as well as information presented at the same time as the target.

context effect: that the ease with which you can remember something is a function of the degree to which the context in which you are trying to retrieve the information matches the context in which you originally encoded it.

deep approach: an approach to learning that emphasies the underlying principles and relationships between details.

digit span: the number of digits that you can correctly repeat back, in the correct order. A measure of working memory capacity.

distinctiveness principle: memory codes are easier to find when they can be easily distinguished from other related codes.

domino principle: the principle that activating one memory code will cause other linked codes to be activated also.

elaborative interrogation: a non-transformational strategy involving turning the facts to be learned into why-questions.

emotional memory: a component of autobiographical memory. The memory domain that holds your memory of how you felt on particular occasions.

encoding: transforming information into a memory code, and placing it in your memory.

environmental aid: a physical object or event that cues memory.

event memory: includes memory for specific events that have happened to you, as well as general event scripts, and a potted summary.

face–name association: is a variant of the keyword method for remembering people's names.

fan effect: because there is only so much activation to go around, the more memory codes that are activated, the less activation each one receives. Retrieval becomes slower and more difficult.

first-letter mnemonic: is a list-learning strategy that uses the initial letters of the items to aid recall. There are two types: acronyms and acrostics.

forgetting: not being able to find a memory code.

frequency effect: a memory code is easier to access the more often it has been activated in the past.

generation strategy: a search strategy that enables you to systematically produce a number of possible recall cues.

goal: your articulation of the target at the beginning of your search. The more specific it is, the more likely your search will be successful, and the more likely you are to recognise that you have indeed reached your target.

graphic organisers: a type of graphic summary appropriate for material that can be expressed hierarchically, that allows the comparison of between-cluster relations.

graphic summaries: summarise the main points of a text in a different format than the straightforward string of statements.

headings: single words or phrases that label sections in a text and help organise it in a hierarchical structure.

highlighting: any way of emphasising key words or phrases, such as underlining, framing, using bold type, or using a coloured marker.

identity memory: includes separate domains for physical features, facial expression, semantic information (e.g. occupation, marital status, address, etc.), visual information (e.g. gender, approximate age, ethnicity, etc.) and names. A component of social memory.

imagery: the use of visual images to encode non-visual information.

internal representation: a neural event in the brain that holds your version of some information event.

keyword method: transforms a word into an image via a keyword – a word derived from the word to be learned, that is imageable. The keyword method is useful for linking pairs of items – a word with its meaning, a capital with its country, a country with its product.

knowledge memory: the memory domain concerned with general, encyclopedic knowledge of the world, and language. Also known as semantic memory, or sometimes, reference memory.

learning style: your predisposition to apply particular encoding strategies.

link method: has no well-learned anchors, but simply links items in a chain of paired items.

list-learning strategies: include three strategies using imagery to link items in a list: the place method, the pegword method and the link method, and two strategies using words to link items: the story method and first-letter mnemonics.

maintenance rehearsal: simple repetition to hold an item in working memory.

maps: graphic summaries that display main ideas in a structured but non-hierarchical format.

matching effect: a memory code is easier to find the more closely the code and retrieval cue match.

memory domain: a part of memory that deals with information of a specific type, and has its own principles of organisation.

mind-mapping: a mapping strategy made famous in a number of books by Tony Buzan.

mnemonic strategies: are aids to memory such as acronyms, acrostics, techniques that link information by creating visual images or making up a story. They are most suitable for information that is not inherently meaningful.

monitoring: strategies to inform you how well you have learned the information in a memory situation so that you can plan your encoding strategies appropriately.

multimedia summaries: graphic summaries that combine pictures and text in an integrated manner. Especially appropriate for demonstrating scientific explanations.

name code: the memory code that contains the person's name. It is only accessible through the semantic codes.

network: the structure of memory – memory codes that are connected to each other.

non-transformational elaboration: elaborating information to make it more memorable by linking it with familiar information that is meaningfully connected.

outcome goals: your objective in carrying out a learning task, in terms of the desired outcome.

outlines: a type of graphic summary appropriate for material that can be expressed hierarchically.

pegword method: is similar to the place method, but uses numbers as pegs or anchors. Images for the numbers are rote-learned by means of a rhyme. The pegword method can be extended using a coding system.

personal memory: the memory domain that holds information about people – yourself and others. Includes information about events and experiences, feelings and beliefs, behaviour and identity. Sometimes called episodic memory.

place method: is traditionally known as the method of loci. Images of items to be remembered are visualised at familiar landmarks, in a set order.

planning memory: memory for intentions that we wish to carry out in the future. Sometimes called prospective memory.

priming effect: a memory code is readier to activate, and so easier to access, when memory codes linked to it have been recently activated.

process goals: specific intermediate objectives that need to be achieved on the way to producing the desired outcome of a learning task.

reading span: a measure of working memory capacity that is related to your ability to understand written and spoken information.

recency effect: a memory code is more readily activated when it has recently been activated.

relational images: visual images that bring together at least two items.

repetition: repeating information is the simplest learning strategy, and is effective because of the frequency effect.

restatement: paraphrasing information in your own words.

retrieval or recall cues: information that prompts your memory search.

retrieving: finding a memory code – transforming it from a data-base memory code into an active working memory code.

script: a generalised outline or composite framework that has been constructed from a number of specific examples.

secondary recall cues: the memory codes whose connections define the trail of your memory search.

self-description: a component of autobiographical memory. The memory domain that holds the information that makes up your 'self' – your identity information.

semantic: the meaning of a word.

semantic codes: memory codes that contain information about a person – their occupation, whether they have a partner, children, etc.

skill memory: the memory domain that deals with motor skills, such as playing a musical instrument, and cognitive skills, such as reading or computer programming.

skimming: skipping speedily through text actively searching for critical information.

social memory: contains your memory for other people – their identity (which itself breaks down into three different types of information), biographical details and memory for their behaviour. A component of personal memory.

spacing effect: repetition is far more effective when it occurs at spaced intervals, rather than at one time.

structural codes: memory codes that contain information about physical features of a person.

study strategies: encoding strategies that help you understand and recall meaningful information, in particular factual information from books or oral presentations.

super-cluster: clusters of codes can be linked to other clusters. To the extent that the connections are strong, the network of clusters can be treated as one cluster.

super-cluster effect: if memory codes are sufficiently well integrated, clusters can be activated as a single unit. Accordingly, even when many memory codes are activated, if they are strongly clustered, retrieval is not hindered.

support strategies: strategies that support your encoding and retrieval skills.

surface approach: an approach to learning that emphasises superficial similarities between details, and is concerned with reproducing information rather than understanding it.

taking notes: strategies that promote the effective selection of important information by restating and reorganising textual material.

target: the memory code you wish to retrieve.

theme: a single word or phrase that unites the bits of information in a cluster.

topical summaries: summarise the main points of a text point by point.

transformational elaboration: elaborating information to make it more memorable by transforming it into an interactive image.

transformational elaborative strategies: strategies that link new information with familiar memory codes through transformation. They include the keyword method and face–name association, which use imagery, and the coding method, which transforms numbers into words.

trigger events: events that trigger intended activities.

visually derived semantic codes: memory codes that contain that information about a person that can be discerned simply by looking at them – for example, their approximate age, their gender, etc.

word span: the number of words you can repeat back in the correct order. A measure of working memory capacity that affects your ability to acquire new and foreign vocabulary.

working memory: that state of memory in which memory codes can be looked at and worked with.

working memory capacity: the amount of information you can hold and work with at one time.

Quick reference 3: Recommended reading

Some general books for the interested reader are:
Baddeley, A *Your Memory: A User's Guide* (New edition) London: Penguin Books, 1994.
Gruneberg, M M and Herrmann, D J *Your Memory for Life!* London: Blandford, 1997.
Higbee, K L *Your Memory: How It Works and How to Improve It* (2nd ed.) Sydney: Prentice Hall Press, 1988.
These authors are all academics in the field of memory research and know what they're talking about. The first two books in particular are very readable.

Books about specific strategies

Mnemonics

There are a number of books available that describe mnemonic strategies, for example:
Buzan, T *Use your Memory* London: BBC, 1974 (reprinted 1984, 1986, 1989).

Since a major value of mnemonic strategies is to acquire foreign languages, it is worth noting that Dr Michael Gruneberg (an academic who has focused on practical applications of memory

research) has written several books using the 'Linkword' system (a keyword strategy) to learn German, Italian, Spanish and French, for example:
Gruneberg, M M *German by Association* Maidenhead: Passport Books, 1994.

Mind Maps

Tony Buzan has written a number of books on mind-mapping, his own version of a mapping strategy. The latest one is called *The Mind Map Book* (London: BBC, 1993), which is very visual (lots of pictures, illustrations, etc.). If you prefer something more strictly factual, you might like his very popular early book, *Use Your Head* (London: BBC, 1974; reprinted 1982, 1984, 1985, 1986, 1987, 1989).

Study skills

There are a number of books available that discuss study strategies, such as:
Winder, J *Learning Success: A Practical Guide for Learners who Want Results* Auckland: ESA Publications Ltd, 1994.
For a more academic approach, there is:
Baine, D *Memory and Instruction* Englewood Cliffs, NJ: Educational Technology Publications, 1986.
Biggs, J B and Moore, P J *The Process of Learning* (3rd ed.) Sydney: Prentice Hall Press, 1993.
This book also discusses learning styles.

Learning styles

Harrison, A F and Bramson, R M *The Art of Thinking* New York: Anchor Press, 1982.

Although this is not strictly about the type of learning styles I have been talking about, this is an interesting and readable book about different styles of thinking. For a more academic discussion about the specific learning styles I have discussed, you could read:

Ramsden, P. (ed.) *Improving Learning: New Perspectives* New York: Nichols Publishing Co., 1988.

For a longer list of helpful books, please do have a look at my website, www.memory-key.com.

I've mentioned several studies in *Perfect Memory Training* and in case you're interested in looking into them in more depth, here are the details in full:

Barsalou, L W 'The content and organisation of autobiographical memories' in Neisser, U & Winograd, E (eds.) *Remembering Reconsidered: Ecological and Traditional Approaches to the Study of Memory* Cambridge: Cambridge University Press, 1988 (193–243)

Bransford, J D, Stein, B S, Shelton, T S and Owings, R A 'Cognition and adaptation: the importance of learning to learn' in Harvey, J (ed.) *Cognition, Social Behaviour and the Environment* New Jersey: Erlbaum, 1981 (93–110)

Broadbent, D E, Cooper, P J and Broadbent M H 'A comparison of hierarchical and matrix retrieval schemes in recall', *Journal of Experimental Psychology: Human Learning and Memory*, 4 (1978), 486–97

Cantor, J and Engle, R W 'Working-memory capacity as long-term memory activation: an individual-differences approach', *Journal of Experimental Psychology: Learning, Memory and Cognition*, 19 (1993), 1101–14

Daneman, M and Carpenter, P A 'Individual differences in working memory and reading', *Journal of Verbal Learning and Verbal Behaviour*, 19 (1980), 450–66

Marks, D F 'Individual differences in the vividness of visual imagery and their effect on function' in Sheehan, P W (ed.) *The*

Function and Nature of Imagery New York: Academic Press, 1972, 83–108

Mayer, R E, Bove, W, Bryman, A, Mars, R and Tapangco, L 'When less is more: meaningful learning from visual and verbal summaries of science textbook lessons', *Journal of Educational Psychology*, 88 (1996), 64–73

McCormick, C B and Levin, J R 'Mnemonic prose-learning strategies' in McDaniel, M A and Pressley, M. (eds.) *Imagery and Related Mnemonic Processes: Theories, Individual Differences, and Applications* New York: Springer-Verlag, 1987 (392–406)

Robinson, D H and Kiewra, K A 'Visual argument: graphic organisers are superior to outlines in improving learning from text', *Journal of Educational Psychology*, 87 (1995), 455–67

Woloshyn, V E, Willoughby, T, Wood, E and Pressley, M 'Elaborative interrogation facilitates adult learning of factual paragraphs', *Journal of Educational Psychology*, 82, (1990), 513–24

Answers to exercises

2.2

1. place(s) you usually post letters at; other cheques you wrote at the same time; any letters you posted in the past three days; other events on the day you should have posted it (the day itself is a cue for these)
2. places where you might know the person from; people with whom the person might be associated
3. searching for occasions on which name might have been spoken: occasions you might have played with her; other people who might have been involved; other (social) occasions on which you might have seen her; searching for places name might have appeared in print: club lists, newsletters, etc.

2.3

1. insurance cheque; action of posting
2. insurance cheque; plumber cheque; action of posting; Monday
3. insurance cheque; plumber cheque; action of posting; corner postbox; walking to postbox after tea; Monday

Goal 3 is most likely to result in recalling posting the cheque
alphabet search problem:
Albania: Tirane; Belgium: Brussels; Chile: Santiago; Denmark: Copenhagen; Ecuador: Quito; Fiji: Suva; Ghana: Accra; Hungary: Budapest; Iraq: Baghdad; Jamaica: Kingston; Kenya: Nairobi; Lebanon: Beirut; Mongolia: Ulan Bator; Nigeria: Lagos; Oman: Muscat; Pakistan: Islamabad; Syria: Damascus; Taiwan: Taipei; Uruguay: Montevideo; Vietnam: Hanoi

Shopping list example:

vegetables: broccoli; cabbage; courgettes, red peppers; tomatoes

fruit: apples; bananas; oranges; kiwi fruit; pears

'cold': cheese; yogurt; fresh soya milk; bacon; margarine

'frozen': frozen peas; frozen beans; frozen blueberries; hash browns; chicken nuggets

'breakfast': tinned fruit; fruit juice; cornflakes; strawberry jam; bread

'baking': eggs; icing sugar; caster sugar; rice flakes; yeast

'noodles, etc.': quick noodles; kidney beans; tacos; rice; pasta

'non-food': toilet paper; tissues; shampoo; washing powder; soap

3.1

There are connections between: 3 & 5; 4 & 6; 7 & 8 & 9; 7 & 10; 7 & 11; 10 & 11; 8 & 12.
You could form a cluster with 7 & 8 & 9 & 10 &11 around the theme *Vivaldi's failure as a priest.*

6.2

Here are some suggestions.

If you're versed in Chinese history, you might pick 478 as the final year of the Song dynasty (knowing historical dates can be very useful for chunking numbers!). Or if you're technically inclined, you might recognise it as the number of a socket used for Intel's Pentium 4 chip. It's a bus route number in Melbourne, and also the number given to one of Mozart's piano quartets. You might also recognise it as a familiar area code.

For 69: maybe you or someone you know was born in 1969, or maybe you have a fondness for the festival at Woodstock! It was also the year Neil Armstrong walked on the moon – indeed, 1969 is a fertile ground for mnemonics.

23: might be remembered in terms of the famous Psalm, or as the number the basketballer Michael Jordan wore. It's also the number of chromosomes in our sex cells. The mathematically inclined might think of it as the ninth prime number or the sixth happy number, or as one of only two integers that can't be expressed as the sum of fewer than 9 cubes of integers! On a more personal note, maybe something memorable happened to you when you were 23, or 23 is part of a familiar address.

6923: as long as you encode the information that the number is backward, you can reverse numbers, and this can be particularly helpful for longer numbers, such as this one. 3296 might be part of a familiar address. It might be familiar to you as the height of a mountain (for example, in the United States, Bear Mountain, Old Rag Mountain, and Robertson Mountain are all 3,296 feet high), or perhaps you're familiar with 3,296 as the number of million litres of sewage that Delhi dumps in the river every day! Probably not, but you take my point I hope – everyone has different interests and pools of knowledge, and the more meaningful numbers you have stored in your database, the more chance you'll have something to use when there's a meaningless number you want to remember.

Also, even if you have no particular interest in remembering odd facts, you'll probably be surprised how many numbers have some sort of association for you, if you get in the habit of searching for them.

4786923: But here we come up against the limits of meaningfulness when it comes to numbers. The extremely numerate might find some means of making this whole number meaningful, but for most of us, this is where you need a coding mnemonic (discussed in chapter ten).

8.3:

theme: 'country'
alternative theme: 'farmwork'

8.4:

1. The first connects the two nouns with a conjunction, the second with a locational preposition, and the third with an interactive preposition. The third is more memorable – not because it's funnier, but because it's interactive.
2. In the first list the noun pairs sound the same. In the second, they look the same. In the third, they are meaningfully connected.

9.3:

1. coding and pegword methods
2. coding mnemonic
3. keyword method
4. place method
5. link or story method

11.1:

1. Retrieval task. Involves memory for other people and memory for personal events (your decisions as to who gets what). You're in a group situation (and the others in the group may help you in recalling items). There will be cues in the shops. But you're probably feeling frazzled, and there is probably some urgency in getting it all done on that occasion.

   It is probably best to make a new list – the act of writing down will help recall the previous action of making a list, as well as relieve the load on working memory, and reduce your stress. Start by writing down all the people you have to get presents for, then try and attach present suggestions. Category labels (chemist's shop; books; clothes, etc.) will help.

2. Retrieval task. Involves memory for specific events. You're in the right environment for retrieving the information (assuming you're at the library), and so there are plenty of cues around. However, the familiarity of the environment also works against you – you need to search for something *distinctive* about your last visit.
   You do this by searching for cues, for example:

   Can you clearly remember the last time you visited the library? No.

   When do you usually go? Before tennis, therefore Monday evening.

   Did you go last week? Yes.

   Can you remember the visit now? No.

   Look at the books you took out on that occasion.

   Can you remember getting them out? Yes.

Now can you remember the visit? Yes.

Do you remember returning your books? No.

Can you remember any other books you returned? Yes.

Try and visualise these books.

Now can you remember the missing book? Yes!

3. Encoding task. Involves planning memory. The information is meaningless. It is presented on an appointment card. You need to remember the information until you have had the appointment. You don't need to remember all the information at one time – you could focus on the day, until the day arrives, and then focus on the time. There may be environmental constraints on the way in which you can encode this information externally (that is, your use of diaries, calendars, etc.).

   Your best strategy probably involves the use of an appropriate external aid (including asking someone to remind you). An appropriate internal strategy would involve linking the appointment with some useful trigger event.

4. Encoding task. Involves knowledge memory. The information is meaningful. It is presented in a written document that is complex, but not difficult I hope! You want to remember the information in order to a) develop expertise in human memory, and/or b) use it to improve your remembering skills. You want to remember the information forever. You only need to remember the meaning, not the exact words. Probably you can schedule your encoding for a time and place that is favourable for attention.

The appropriate strategy (set of strategies, really, because a number would need to be involved in a task as complex as this) involves building understanding through multiple connections. You need to choose study strategies that encourage you to search for the underlying relationships, integrate separate sections of text, etc.

Index

ALSO AVAILABLE IN RANDOM HOUSE BOOKS

Perfect Brain Training

Philip Carter

All you need to boost your brainpower

- Do you sometimes find yourself getting confused or forgetting things?
- Are you worried that your thinking is not as sharp as it used to be?
- Do you want a simple way to improve your brainpower?

Perfect Brain Training is essential reading for anyone who wants to improve their mental agility. Containing a series of fun interactive workouts, it helps you develop every aspect of your thinking skills, from logical deduction and creative problem solving to memory power and verbal dexterity. With advice to help you put together an effective training programme and tests so that you can track your progress, *Perfect Brain Training* has everything you need to make the most of your potential.

The *Perfect* series is a range of practical guides that give clear and straightforward advice on everything from getting your first job to choosing your baby's name. Written by experienced authors offering tried-and-tested tips, each book contains all you need to get it right first time.

ALSO AVAILABLE IN RANDOM HOUSE BOOKS

Perfect Psychometric Test Results

Joanna Moutafi and Ian Newcombe

All you need to get it right first time

- Have you been asked to sit a psychometric test?
- Do you want guidance on the sorts of questions you'll be asked?
- Do you want to make sure you perform to the best of your abilities?

Perfect Psychometric Test Results is an essential guide for anyone who wants to secure their ideal job. Written by a team from Kenexa, one of the UK's leading compilers of psychometric tests, it explains how each test works, gives helpful pointers on how to get ready, and provides professionally constructed sample questions for you to try out at home. It also contains an in-depth section on online testing – the route that more and more recruiters are choosing to take. Whether you're a graduate looking to take the first step on the career ladder, or you're planning an all-important job change, *Perfect Psychometric Test Results* has everything you need to make sure you stand out from the competition.

BOOKS

Order more titles in the *Perfect* series from your local bookshop, or have them delivered direct to your door by Bookpost.

	Title	Author	ISBN	Price
☐	Perfect Answers to Interview Questions	Max Eggert	9781905211722	£7.99
☐	Perfect Babies' Names	Rosalind Fergusson	9781905211661	£5.99
☐	Perfect Brain Training	Philip Carter	9781847945549	£6.99
☐	Perfect Calorie Counting	Kate Santon	9781847945181	£6.99
☐	Perfect CV	Max Eggert	9781905211739	£7.99
☐	Perfect Interview	Max Eggert	9781905211746	£7.99
☐	Perfect Numerical Test Results	Joanna Moutafi and Ian Newcombe	9781905211333	£7.99
☐	Perfect Personality Profiles	Helen Baron	9781905211821	£7.99
☐	Perfect Presentations	Andrew Leigh and Michael Maynard	9781847945518	£6.99
☐	Perfect Psychometric Test Results	Joanna Moutafi and Ian Newcombe	9781905211678	£7.99
☐	Perfect Pub Quiz	David Pickering	9781905211692	£6.99
☐	Perfect Punctuation	Stephen Curtis	9781905211685	£5.99
☐	Perfect Readings for Weddings	Jonathan Law	9781905211098	£6.99
☐	Perfect Written English	Chris West	9781847945037	£6.99

Free post and packing
Overseas customers allow £2 per paperback

Phone: 01624 677237

Post: Random House Books
c/o Bookpost, PO Box 29, Douglas, Isle of Man IM99 1BQ

Fax: 01624 670 923

email: bookshop@enterprise.net

Cheques (payable to Bookpost) and credit cards accepted

Prices and availability subject to change without notice.
Allow 28 days for delivery.
When placing your order, please state if you do not wish to receive any additional information.

www.randomhouse.co.uk